Buddha Śākyamuni

Guru Padmasambhava

Longchen Rabjam Drimé Özer

༄༅།།དཔལ་གསོ་སྦྱོར་གསུམ་ལས་བསམ་གཏན་དཔལ་གསོའི་
རྩ་བ་དང་འགྲེལ་པ་ཤིང་རྟ་རྣམ་པར་དག་པ་
ཞེས་བྱ་བ་བཞུགས་སོ།།

པོད་ཀུ་པའི་སྒྲ་བསྒྱུར་མཐུན་ཚོགས་ནས་
སྒྲ་བསྒྱུར་ཞུས།

The Padmakara Translation Group gratefully acknowledges
the generous support of the Tsadra Foundation in sponsoring
the translation and preparation of this book.

Finding Rest in Meditation

The Trilogy of Rest, Volume 2

Longchenpa

TRANSLATED BY

The Padmakara Translation Group

SHAMBHALA

Shambhala Publications, Inc.
4720 Walnut Street
Boulder, Colorado 80301
www.shambhala.com

© 2018 by Association Padmakara
Paperback edition published 2020

Front cover art: Detail of thangka of Milarepa, Tibet, 19. Jh.; inv. no. IId 13769,
Essen collection; Photographer: Omar Lemke © Museum der Kulturen Basel,
Switzerland; All rights reserved.
Back cover art: Thangka of Longchenpa. Image courtesy of Matthieu Ricard.

9 8 7 6 5 4 3 2 1

First paperback edition
Printed in the United States of America

⊛ This edition is printed on acid-free paper that meets the American
National Standards Institute z39.48 Standard.
♻ This book is printed on 30% postconsumer recycled paper.
For more information please visit www.shambhala.com.
Shambhala Publications is distributed worldwide by Penguin Random
House, Inc., and its subsidiaries.

THE LIBRARY OF CONGRESS CATALOGUES THE PREVIOUS EDITION
OF THIS BOOK AS FOLLOWS:

Names: Klong-chen-pa Dri-med-'od-zer, 1308–1363, author. | Klong-chen-pa Dri-med-'od-zer,
1308–1363. Sems nyid ngal gso. English. | Klong-chen-pa Dri-med-'od-zer, 1308–1363.
Bsam gtan ngal gso. English. | Klong-chen-pa Dri-med-'od-zer, 1308–1363.
Sgyu ma ngal gso. English. | Comité de traduction Padmakara, translator.
Title: Trilogy of rest / Longchen Rabjam; translated by the Padmakara Translation Group.
Description: First edition. | Boulder: Shambhala, 2017– |
Includes bibliographical references and index.
Identifiers: LCCN 2017009896 | ISBN 9781611805161 (hardback: v. 1) / ISBN 9781611807523
(pbk.: alk. paper: v. 1) | ISBN 9781611805529 (hardback: v. 2) / ISBN 9781611807530 (pbk.: alk.
paper: v. 2) | ISBN 9781611805925 (hardback: v. 3) / 9781611807547 (pbk.: alk. paper: v. 3)
Subjects: LCSH: Rdzogs-chen—Early works to 1800. | BISAC: RELIGION / Buddhism /
Tibetan. | RELIGION / Buddhism / Sacred Writings. | RELIGION / Buddhism /
Rituals & Practice.
Classification: LCC BQ7662.4 .K5465 2017 | DDC 294.3/420423—dc23
LC record available at https://lccn.loc.gov/2017009896

CONTENTS

Foreword

Alak Zenkar Rinpoche

Supreme among the vast array of pith instructions,
Bringing into one epitome
The crucial points without exception of the Tripitaka
And the four classes of Tantra,
These volumes are the summit of a myriad treatises
That heal and that protect,
A perfect chariot of teaching clear and unsurpassed,
The supreme means whereby
The minds of those who wander in the triple world,
Find rest in freedom.

Priceless in this universe,
This scripture is the image of the speech of Longchen,
Dharma king from Samyé, who in times to come
Will have the name of the Victorious Merudipa.
It is a beauteous mirror formed of flawless crystal
That reveals the sense of the essential lore
Of the three yogas and nine stages of the Mahāyāna,
Passed down by word of mouth and in the precious treasures,
Rich patrimony of the line of knowledge-holders
Of the Ancient Translations.

Your aspiration first arose
Upon the shoulders of the eastern hills

And now your translation in a foreign tongue
Shines like the day-creating sun
Assisted by the light of publication's wizardry.
I celebrate its coming,
The sweet friend of the lotus of the Buddha's doctrine.

From the smiling blossom of delight and happiness
There falls such honeyed nectar of rejoicing
That, not waiting for the songs of the applauding bees,
I cannot help but pour out my congratulation.

I who have grown old beneath this canopy of joy,
This great refulgence of the sunlight
Of the doctrine of the powerful Sage,
Cannot but speak my praises of your wish
To be of service to his teaching.

Therefore may this lucid textual explanation,
Indeed a health-sustaining herb
For teachings of the Ancient Translation School
And source of glorious sustenance for many beings,
Increase a hundred, thousand, millionfold
And be widely spread and propagated.

With excellent aspiration and activity for the Buddha's doctrine in general and especially for the orally transmitted and treasure teachings of the Ancient Tradition of the Great Secret, the Padmakara translators have rendered into English the root texts of the Trilogy of Rest, which are now published together with their autocommentaries, the spotlessly clear exposition of the mighty Conqueror Longchen Rabjam. With joy and admiration, I, Thubten Nyima, join my hands at my heart and offer flowers of rejoicing. Written in the fragrant city of Chengdu on the twelfth day of the seventh month, in the year 2017.

Translators' Introduction

F*INDING REST IN MEDITATION*[1] is the second part of the Trilogy of Rest of Longchen Rabjam Drimé Özer. Details of the life and times of Longchenpa, as he is more frequently known, together with a general description of his writings are to be found in the introduction to the first part of the trilogy, *Finding Rest in the Nature of the Mind*,[2] and there is no need to repeat them here. It is sufficient to remind the reader that the Trilogy of Rest—or, more literally, the Three Cycles on Rest[3]—is composed not of three books but of three groups of texts, each of which comprises a root text in verse, an autocommentary called a "chariot," a brief synopsis called a "garland," and an essential instruction or "guide to practice."[4] Finally, the trilogy as a whole is rounded off with a general presentation entitled *An Ocean of Elegant Explanations*.[5]

For reasons of time and practicality, only the root texts and the autocommentaries have figured in the present translation project. Moreover, as was explained in the translators' introduction to *Finding Rest in the Nature of the Mind*, a complete translation of *The Great Chariot*,[6] the immense autocommentary to that work, replete as it is with many long and difficult citations from the sūtras and tantras, was not made. Instead a selection of important passages representative of Longchenpa's thought were excerpted, translated, and supplied as an accompaniment to the root text. By contrast, *The Chariot of Surpassing Purity*,[7] the autocommentary to *Finding Rest in Meditation*, being compendious and fairly straightforward, has been translated in full in the present volume.

Unlike the Seven Great Treasures, only six of which were listed as separate items in Longchenpa's own catalog, and which seem to have been grouped together as a single entity by later tradition owing to the similarity of their names, the three clusters of texts that compose the Trilogy of Rest were explicitly compiled into a single collection by the author himself. Yet despite Longchenpa's evident intention to group the three sections of his trilogy together, there are reasons for thinking that they were not composed systematically as a single literary entity.

It is clear, for instance, that the components of the trilogy were not written in the order given in the general presentation. For while *Finding Rest in the Nature of the Mind* and its commentary *The Great Chariot* were undoubtedly composed first, being cited in the subsequent texts, internal evidence shows that at least the autocommentary to *Finding Rest in Meditation* was composed after the autocommentary to *Finding Rest in Illusion*,[8] which is the third part of the trilogy.

The titles of the three root texts, as well as of the trilogy itself, do indeed suggest that the entire collection was conceived and composed together around the single unifying theme of "rest"—the reposeful state of enlightenment in which beings find comfort and relief from their interminable wanderings in saṃsāra. "Today," Longchenpa announces in the general prologue, "I will bring rest to their exhausted minds." But whereas this idea figures prominently in *Finding Rest in the Nature of the Mind*, appearing in the concluding lines of each of its thirteen chapters, it does not occur at all in the second and third sections of the trilogy, except in the titles of their root texts. It is only in the general presentation of the trilogy, and through a detailed explanation of the titles of the root texts, that Longchenpa explicitly extends to the entire collection a metaphor that, as a self-evident poetic feature, is present only in the first part.

Longchenpa tells us that he has arranged his trilogy according to the well-known formula of ground, path, and action. Clearly, the ground or view is supplied by *Finding Rest in the Nature of the Mind*, which, together with its long autocommentary, is a comprehensive *lamrim* or exposition of the stages of the Buddhist path, culminating in the teachings of the Great Perfection. And it looks very much as though the author wished to supplement his exposition by the addition of two shorter auxiliary cycles of texts that explain, first, how practitioners are to engage in meditation on the basis of such a ground or view and, second, how they should deal with the experiences of life in the postmeditation period. Perhaps it was in order to impart a sense of literary unity to the entire compilation therefore that Longchenpa took an idea figuring strongly in both the title and contents of the first section and extended it to the two root texts that followed—a procedure the artificiality of which is further suggested by the trouble taken in the general presentation to explain and justify the titles thus devised.

In his discussion of the title *Finding Rest in Meditation*, Longchenpa begins by considering the objection that since meditative absorption is a state in which there is no movement of thought, it is already and by definition a state of perfect rest. To speak of finding rest in it is therefore redundant and tautological—absurdly implying that there is some aspect of meditation that is not restful. In reply to this objection, Lonchenpa makes a distinction between what he calls "worldly" and "transworldly" meditation.

It should be understood that the meditation referred to here is not the kind of analytical meditation in which an idea is subjected to intellectual analysis, but the practice of calm abiding, or *śamatha*, the aim of which is to achieve a clear and perfectly focused state of mental stillness. As the basis for all other forms of mental and spiritual training, this kind of meditation was pursued with zeal in practically all the religious and philosophical traditions of ancient India, Buddhist and non-Buddhist.

It should be noticed on the other hand that, however important śamatha may be as a tool for training the mind and developing its powers, it is, soteriologically speaking, a neutral force. It may be productive of quite different results depending on the view or philosophical position with which it is conjoined. At the risk of oversimplification, we may say that the brāhmanical schools of India, specifically those based on the Upanishads and the Vedanta, affirm the existence of an eternal, spiritual, and blissful self or *ātman*, which is the essential core of living beings. Deliverance or *mokṣa*, the culmination of the spiritual path, consists in the knowledge and realization of the ātman as one's innermost essence or true self, and in the discovery that it is identical with Brahman, the eternal, self-existent principle and source of the universe.

The Buddhist view diverges radically from this position. The Buddha pointedly denied the existence of an eternal self or ātman as well as the existence of an eternal universal creator. And he declared that it is precisely the clinging to such a supposed self that gives rise to action, setting in motion and maintaining the unending cycle of saṃsāric existence. The mistaken apprehension of a self is thus the antithesis of the path to liberation. From the Buddhist point of view, a mastery of śamatha informed by a belief in ātman may well result in the highest states of celestial bliss for immense lapses of time. But however pure and protracted these states may be in the form and formless realms, they do not escape the law of impermanence. Founded on a belief in self, they too are the effects of action—even the subtle action of concentrated absorption—and when their causes are exhausted, they must at length cease. They are consequently marred by the fundamental dissatisfaction that is the hallmark of saṃsāric existence. By contrast, it is only when the supposedly independent and permanent self is shown to be nonexistent, and when clinging to it is consequently dissipated, that freedom from saṃsāra is possible. Therefore, although the mastery of śamatha is indeed an indispensable tool in spiritual endeavor, it must, if it is to result in liberation, be conjoined with the view of no-self, the wisdom of emptiness, the profound insight of vipaśyanā.

This is the reason for Longchenpa's distinction, mentioned earlier, between worldly and transworldly meditation. The former, the practice of śamatha uninformed by wisdom, is defined as "a concentration that is qualified by clarity and no-thought and is experienced in the three realms of saṃsāra."[9] This may result in the temporary suppression of manifest suffering, albeit for very long periods, but the solution is not definitive. When the causes of celestial bliss are exhausted, the mind inevitably falls prey to karmic evolution and must resume its wanderings in saṃsāra, through states of manifest or latent suffering, without ever a hope of finding a state of definitive rest. Transworldly meditation, on the other hand, occurs when calm abiding is joined with the wisdom of emptiness. Thus empowered, the mind is able to uproot its mistaken clinging to self. The root of existence is severed and the weariness of perpetual movement is at long last brought to an end. Only the wisdom that realizes no-self is able to bring peace and refreshment to the exhausted minds of beings. In short, Longchenpa says, to find rest in meditation is to discover the liberation that comes exclusively through the union of śamatha and vipaśyanā.[10]

This, therefore, is the subject of the present text, in which the wisdom of vipaśyanā is presented in terms of the teachings of the Great Perfection, the aim of which is to recognize the nature of the mind and to stabilize and prolong this recognition so as to elicit the full manifestation or actualization of the mind's intrinsically and primordially enlightened state. To this end, *Finding Rest in Meditation* addresses three topics or "vajra points": first, a discussion of the conditions, geographical and otherwise, suitable for retreat in solitude; second, a consideration of the kinds of people liable to succeed in such endeavors; and third, a general presentation of the practices concerned, together with advice on how to intensify their effects and correct mistakes.

Longchenpa describes his text as a series of essential pith instructions. Rather than a systematic exposition of meditation as such, it is a series of particular points of advice directed to experienced practitioners. This is an important point. The instructions contained in this book are not addressed to the uninitiated reader, who would be ill advised to embark on any of the practices described without considerable preparation and the expert guidance of a qualified master. It is, however, of universal interest inasmuch as all the explanations it contains, clear and uncluttered as they are, reflect Longchenpa's own preoccupations and his own findings.

As he says in the general prologue and on several occasions subsequently, his teaching has the backing, and is therefore the record, of his own personal experience. Therefore, even though the text is not a manual of instructions addressed to the general public, we are nevertheless compensated by the light it throws on the character of its author. It is profoundly inspiring and even thrilling thus to catch a glimpse of Longchenpa's personal practice and to have some idea of the single-pointed determination and diligence, as well as the extraordinary ability, that supported it.

THE FIRST VAJRA POINT: A PLACE FOR MEDITATION

The intensive practice of meditation naturally implies retreat in solitude. Therefore, the first vajra point of *Finding Rest in Meditation* contains advice on how to select locations best suited to the cultivation of śamatha and vipaśyanā. In his exposition, Longchenpa refers to two texts: the *Profound Practice of Yoga in the Four Seasons*[11] ascribed to the Dzogchen patriarch Garab Dorje, and the *Garland of the Fortress of Views*[12] by Guru Padmasambhava. In both these texts it is axiomatic that successful practice depends on the cultivation of propitious states of mind, which are in turn strongly influenced by the practitioner's physical condition as well as by the outer environment. The right place, a correct diet, and clothing appropriate to the season are all important elements contributing to a successful practice. For example, lightly built structures high in the mountains, which are cool and airy and command a vast and open view, are best suited to the cultivation of vipaśyanā, whereas quiet, low-lying, forested areas or enclosed valleys are propitious for the inward orientation of calm abiding.

Longchenpa also adverts to more subtle dimensions connected with the atmosphere and "feel" of certain places, and he devotes some time to considering the effects of local spirits on the minds of practitioners. Those already well established in meditative concentration will not be unduly disturbed by ghostly presences lingering in the vicinity of charnel grounds or by the spirits and other nonhuman entities that congregate in eerie and uncanny places: rocky crags, lonely lakes, solitary trees, and so on. Beginners, on the other hand, are easily disturbed and are wise to steer clear of such environments. Aspiring practitioners are advised to choose their retreat locations with special care and, before committing themselves, to spend as much as two weeks in assessing the effects a locality may have on their minds. They should be careful to avoid places that are found to provoke agitation and distraction or else dullness and sleepiness and especially environments that seem to induce morose and depressed states of mind that might lead to discouragement and the eventual abandonment of the practice. By contrast, pure, unpolluted, wholesome places, especially when associated with the practice of great meditators of the past, are to be prized. Anyone who has spent time with Tibetan lamas and practitioners will have observed the sensitivity with which they react to landscape and local environment, and the exactitude with which they examine possible places of practice.

THE SECOND VAJRA POINT: THE MEDITATOR

Longchenpa's distinction between worldly and transworldly meditation and the bearing this has on his advice for practitioners—the subject of the second vajra topic—may be brought into clearer focus by briefly referring to the traditional division of spiritual adepts into three groups or scopes. Unlike beings of the first scope, who misguidedly pursue states of permanent happiness in the upper realms of saṃsāra, practitioners of the second scope understand that all saṃsāric states, whether high or low, are transient and unable to provide the definitive relief from suffering that they seek. In search of liberation, therefore, they turn from saṃsāra altogether. The definitive rejection of saṃsāra, or renunciation, marks the beginning of the specifically Buddhist path. Traditionally expressed in terms of a "going forth into homelessness," renunciation has naturally found its chief expression, down the centuries, in a way of life that, for better or worse, has been identified in English as "monastic." As an all-embracing ethical discipline, however, that involves a profound reassessment of the personal relationships and attachments, the hopes and fears that make up the fabric of ordinary worldly life, renunciation is in fact incumbent on all Buddhist practitioners, whether clerics or laypeople, and is the indispensable basis of any authentic and serious practice. Challenging and revolutionary as this reorientation of personal values is, it derives from nothing more than an attentive observation of life itself. It grows from an awareness of life's manifest sorrows: birth, sickness, aging, and death, meeting with what one fears, the loss of what one loves—the endless tale of human misery that, even if punctuated by temporary happiness and ephemeral pleasure, is as recurrent as it is inescapable. And yet such are the self-protective mechanisms of the human psyche that, through forgetfulness and make believe, and a pathetic resolve to "remember only the good times," it habitually insulates itself from its real predicament. It should therefore come as no surprise that throughout his text, and particularly in the second vajra point, Longchenpa repeatedly insists on the need for practitioners to cultivate a persistent sense of sadness and weariness with regard to saṃsāric existence.

We have seen that liberation cannot be achieved without the cutting of saṃsāra's root: the mistaken clinging to the reality of a personal self and of phenomena. For this to happen, a profound realization of emptiness is indispensable. This in turn is unattainable without proficiency in concentration, and for the development of concentration, the wholesome environment of discipline and pure ethics is traditionally regarded as a sine qua non. Pure ethics, therefore, as articulated in the three systems of vows—the monastic and lay vows of *prātimokṣa* or individual liberation, the vows of the bodhisattva path, and the pledges of the Vajrayāna—are an intrinsic feature of the Mahāyāna Buddhist path. As Longchenpa says, all practices geared to the freedom of enlightenment necessarily imply the taking of vows. Without the vows, there is no danger of downfalls, of course, but neither is there any possibility of accomplishment. The destruction and the reaping of a harvest are equally precluded by the absence of a field.

Bringing together the three sets of vows as components of a single path is a matter of some complexity. Longchenpa therefore devotes a large part of the second vajra point to the elucidation of this question and in so doing delineates what would later be regarded as the official position of the Nyingma school.[13] The task at hand is to explain how the apparently contradictory injunctions of the three sets of vows are to be understood and practiced together by a single person. Longchenpa deals with the matter in terms of six principles, the point of which is to show that the inner purpose of all the vows is essentially the same. As the higher vows are successively received, the lower vows are transmuted and enhanced, with the result that, although the external aspects of the lower vows persist, the vows themselves are not contravened by the implementation of the higher commitments.

Longchenpa is particularly concerned to show how the monastic vow of celibacy can be squared with the practices associated with the third initiation of the Vajrayāna. By invoking the six principles just mentioned, he distinguishes between the *śrāvaka* monk (who remains at the level of the prātimokṣa ordination) and the Vajrayāna monk, whose vows have been enhanced through the reception of bodhichitta vows and the samayas of tantric empowerment, and whose mind has been matured through the yogas of the generation and perfection stages. Externally, the śrāvaka monk and the Vajrayāna monk may appear to be on the same level, but in reality they are quite different. And an action that is proscribed for the former may be both appropriate and a source of great merit for the latter.

Obviously, such questions become an issue only for practitioners who are already far advanced along the path and who are actually able to practice the yogas of the third empowerment— which would of course have been the case for Longchenpa himself. The subject nevertheless remains at least of speculative interest for others, and it is no doubt also with a view to allaying the doubts of less experienced practitioners that Longchenpa discusses the matter here.

The rest of the second vajra point addresses more immediate issues. One striking point that Longchenpa makes is that those who are training on the path should avoid being distracted by mistaken altruism: the deluded idea that one can be of actual benefit to others—presumably in the role of a guru or spiritual guide—before one has gained genuine accomplishment for oneself. Now is the time, he says, for self-training and the securing of one's own deliverance. It is only when one has gained genuine realization and possesses, for instance, a clairvoyant insight into the needs of others that one is in a position to provide effective help and guidance. To act otherwise is nothing but dissipation and self-deception, a source of danger to others, and a waste of valuable time. Longchenpa tells his readers to be honest with themselves. "If now you were to die," he asks, "how would you fare?" If one is unable to manage one's own destiny at such a crucial juncture, it is absurd to pretend that one can be an authentic guide for others. In the moment of intensive self-training, therefore, one's concern for others should be mainly expressed in terms of sincere aspiration and prayer.

THE THIRD VAJRA POINT: INSTRUCTIONS FOR THE PRACTICE

The third and longest of the three vajra points is a discussion of the practice itself. It is a fully elaborated treatise in its own right, consisting of preamble, main subject, and concluding instructions. The subject matter is more complex and systematic here than in the previous sections of the book and is marked off by headings and subheadings that consequently assume the character of a structural outline, or *sabche*. This being so, we have extracted them in slightly simplified form and listed them, with indentations and indications of textual level, as a separate document in an appendix. The interested reader will thus be able to appreciate at a glance the manner in which this important section of the book unfolds.

Finding Rest in Meditation, as its subtitle declares, is a teaching of the Great Perfection. This system of instructions is regarded in the Nyingma school as the summit of the Buddhist path, in relation to which all other teachings, of the Śrāvakayāna and Mahāyāna, the sūtras and the tantras, are considered as preliminaries and preparations. Longchenpa classifies these preliminaries as outer, particular, and superior. The outer preliminares are the understanding of impermanence, and the feelings of disenchantment with saṃsāra culminating in the attitude of renunciation, that are characteristic of practitioners of the second scope. The particular preliminaries correspond to the training of the mind and the cultivation of compassion leading to the generation of relative and ultimate bodhichitta. They correspond, in other words, to the sūtra teachings of the Mahāyāna, which, it may be recalled, belong to the sphere of beings of the third scope. Finally, the superior preliminaries comprise the generation and perfection stage practices of the Vajrayāna together with guru yoga.

The visualization of deities and the training on the channels, winds, and essence drops of the subtle body together with the practice of guru yoga, are thus essential preparations for the path of the Great Perfection. With this in mind, Longchenpa prefaces his main exposition with a brief discussion of the tantras. He explains, for example, the number, sequence, and effects of the four empowerments and gives brief instructions on mantra recitation. He succinctly explains that the purpose of the generation stage, in other words, the visualization on the relative level of deities and so forth, is the elimination of ordinary thought and the purification and transformation of one's experience of the world—the aggregates, the elements, and the seven consciousnesses—into the perception of a buddha field. Subsequently, through the implementation of the perfection stage, the discursive activity of the ordinary mind is made to subside completely. The superior preliminaries are in turn completed by the all-important practice of guru yoga, for "the teacher is the root of all paths and the source of all accomplishment." In this way, Longchenpa declares, one may embark without error on the path to liberation without fear of obstacles or delay. "Nowadays," he concludes, "many people meditate on this path without implementing these preliminaries. This, however, is a mistake."

When Longchenpa finally comes to the main teachings, he does not provide us, as one might have expected, with a formal exposition of what are usually regarded as the Great Perfection's two highest practices: *trekchö* and *thögal*. Instead, he prescribes "skillful means of concentration" on bliss, luminosity, and the absence of discursive thought, through which the fundamental nature of the mind—instead of being merely described—is made to appear in actual experience. Thanks, he says, to these skillful means, "luminous primordial wisdom, free from all elaboration, will arise, coemergent, uncontrived." He goes on to say that bliss corresponds to the essence drops, luminosity to the winds or breath, and no-thought to the subtle channels. But although these techniques are thus described in terms redolent of the perfection stage practices, they nevertheless belong to the Great Perfection tradition as expounded by such masters as Garab Dorje and Śrī Siṃha. Longchenpa states very clearly, moreover, that the practices of bliss, luminosity, and no-thought are not ends in themselves. Their purpose is to serve as the triggers that, in conjunction with genuine devotion to the teacher from whom the practitioner has received the all-important pith instructions, directly induce the realization of the mind's nature. The fact that these techniques are of a completely different order compared to the experience that they are expected to provoke is of no significance. Fire and its fuel are also two completely different entities, and yet it is thanks to the indispensable presence of wood that fire occurs.

Although the practices based on bliss, luminosity, and no-thought are explained in some detail, the largest part of the third vajra point is devoted to supplementary clarifications, which are basically of two kinds. There is first a discussion of possible false trails in the three practices just mentioned, together with a description of antidotes prescribed according to three levels of practitioner.

This is followed by a further series of instructions whereby the experiences of bliss, luminosity, and no-thought may be intensified. It will be evident that the practices prescribed in this section, as well as the remedial exercises given in the previous section, are addressed to yogis who are already well versed in such techniques. It would be extremely foolish to imagine that this section of the text constitutes a manual of instructions for the general reader. Occasionally, Longchenpa refers to his instructions as secret, and by this he seems to mean that the practices concerned are being alluded to only partially and indirectly. They presuppose an already considerable knowledge and require further instructions from a qualified master.

But if general readers and beginners in meditation are unable to embark immediately on the path that Longchenpa describes in this section of the text, it is nevertheless an inspiring account of practices to which one might aspire and which, thanks to the instructions received from a qualified master, one may eventually be able to implement.

Acknowledgments

In the preparation of this second part of the Trilogy of Rest, we are once again indebted to our teacher, Pema Wangyal Rinpoche, without whose inspiration and support this translation could never have been made. We are also extremely grateful to Khenchen Pema Sherab of Namdroling Monastery, Bylakuppe, India, who with great patience answered our queries and clarified many difficult points. We have done our best to follow his instructions but acknowledge as our own whatever mistakes and shortcomings may have occurred. This translation was made by Helena Blankleder and Wulstan Fletcher of the Padmakara Translation Group.

Dordogne
June 5, 2017

PART ONE

FINDING REST IN MEDITATION

A Teaching of the Great Perfection

IN SANSKRIT
Mahāsandhidhyānaviśrāntanāma

IN TIBETAN
rDzogs pa chen po bsam gtan ngal gso zhes bya ba

PROLOGUE

Primordial nature,
Pure and vast expanse like space itself,
Supreme reality, unmoving,
Utterly devoid of all elaboration,
Clear and lucent nature of the mind itself,
The essence of enlightenment—
In seeing this unmoving and unchanging perfect ground,
I bow in homage.

That the surpassing wonder of the Conqueror's mind
Be realized—primal wisdom, self-cognizing—
I distilled the essence of the tantras, commentaries, and pith
    instructions.
Pay heed! I shall explain them in the light of my experience.

On mountain peaks and lake isles, or in forest groves,
Congenial to the mind in the four seasons of the year,
With single-pointed concentration, serene, unmoving,
Meditate on luminosity devoid of mind's construction.
Depending on three things is this accomplished:
The place, the persons, and the practices they implement.

1. The First Vajra Point

Concerning the Place of Practice

---

1. First, the place we shall consider.
This should be a pleasant solitude
Amenable for practice in the year's four seasons.
In summer you should meditate
In regions that are cool and in cool habitations,
In snowy places, mountaintops,
In shelters made of bamboo, reeds, or grass.
In autumn you should stay in regions and in dwellings where
The cold and heat are of an equal strength,
In places such as woodlands, hillsides, rocky forts,
With corresponding conduct, food, and clothing.
In wintertime, you should adapt your bedding, food, and dress
And live in dwellings that are warm and in low-lying regions:
Forests, caverns, houses made of earth.
In spring it's most important to retire
To mountains, forests, islands, and to dwell in shelters
Where the heat and cold are balanced,
With food and dress and conduct all in harmony.

2. The external and internal cycles of dependence coincide.
Therefore, stay in pleasant solitudes, in places of delight.
Since on mountain heights the mind is clear and vast,
These regions, where all mental dullness clarifies,
Are beneficial to the practice of the generation stage.
In snowy lands, the mind is bright

With lucid concentration.
These places are propitious for the practice of deep insight,
For here there are few obstacles.
In forest groves, the mind grows calm
And mental stillness manifests.
These are places where one trains in calm abiding
And where mental bliss grows strong.
At the foot of rocky crags, a sense of transience
And a weary sorrow with saṃsāra strengthens.
The clear and powerful union
Of calm abiding and deep insight is achieved.
On riverbanks, the mind's imagination is curtailed.
Sorrow at saṃsāra and the decisive wish
To part from it will rapidly develop.
Charnel grounds are powerful places
Where accomplishment is swift.
Such places, it is taught, are most propitious
For any of the practices of generation and perfection.

3. In towns and markets, empty houses, lonely trees,
Where human beings congregate or elves and spirits pass,
Beginners are distracted and are hindered in their practice.
For those who have stability,
Such places are propitious and supremely praised.
Lonely temples, offering shrines,
Where *gyalgong* spirits dwell, are places where
The mind does not find rest
And many thoughts of enmity arise.
In places such as caverns in the earth,
Which are abodes of *senmo* hags,
Desire arises and an extreme dullness or an
 agitation of the mind.
Lonely trees are haunts of *mamo*s and of ḍākinīs;
Cliffs and promontories are lairs
Of *theurang* wights and wild, ferocious *tsen*.

All such places, it is said, provoke wild agitation
In the mind and many obstacles.
In *haunts* of outcasts, nāgas, *nyen* wraiths, spirits of the place,
On lakeside, grassy heath, in woodland wilds,
In valleys strewn with healing herbs,
Adorned with flowers and fruit and berry-bearing trees,
All pleasing to the mind, at first one is content,
But later many obstacles befall.

4. In brief, in those localities and dwellings
That at first seem pleasant but with familiarity
Lose their charm, only slight accomplishment is gained.
But places that at first seem fearful and forbidding
Yet turn to good as you grow used to them
Are of great power, and great accomplishment is swift to come,
While obstacles do not occur.
All other places, being neutral, neither benefit nor harm.

5. Since in dependence on your dwelling place
Your inner mind is changed, and virtuous practice
Thrives or languishes, to ponder thus your dwelling
Is a point, so it is said, of high importance.

6. There are, in sum, four kinds of dwelling place
According to the four activities.
In places suitable for pacifying, the mind is focused naturally.
Places suitable for increase are delightful,
Filled with splendor and magnificence.
Places that are ravishing and stimulate attachment
Are suited to the action of attracting.
Places suited to the fierce activity
Provoke anxiety and panic fear
There are in fact unnumbered subdivisions of such places.
But here, as aids to concentration,
Places suitable for pacifying are the best.

The others, here, are not considered
For fear of great prolixity.

7. A meditation shelter in a peaceful place
Should be set apart in solitude, in a site that is congenial.
A very open, spacious place where all around
One sees the sky is most conducive.

8. The dark house for the nighttime yoga
Has two sets of walls.
In the center of an inner, elevated room,
Your headrest should be in the north,
As when the Buddha passed into nirvāṇa.
For the daytime yoga in the light,
The hermitage should have a vast expanse in front
With open sky and distant views
Of snowy mountains, falling water,
Woods, and valleys.
In such a place the mind is clear and limpid,
And heat and cold should be in equilibrium.

9. For the practice of abiding in tranquillity,
A hermitage enclosed is most propitious
For the natural rising of the state of mental calm.
When practicing deep insight,
A spacious place that has a vast and open view
Is most important.
It should always be a pleasant place
Appropriate to the season.

10. Low-lying, darksome places such as forests and ravines
Are places fit for calm abiding.
High lands, such as snowy mountains,
Are the places for deep insight.
It is important thus to know these differences.

11. In brief, the places and the hermitages
Where you feel a sadness for saṃsāra
And the wish to free yourself,
Locations where your mind, reined in,
Rests in the present and your concentration grows—
These are sites connecting you to virtue.
You should live in such environments
Resembling the place of Buddha's own enlightenment.
Places where your virtue lessens and defilement grows,
Where you fall beneath the influence
Of the distracting busyness of life,
Are demonic dens of evil deeds avoided by the wise.
Padma, self-arisen, has explained them thus,
And those who wish for freedom should take heed.

This completes the first vajra point of *Finding Rest in Meditation,
a Teaching of the Great Perfection.*

2. The Second Vajra Point

Concerning Those Who Practice Meditation

1. Now persons who engage in practice
Should have diligence and faith
And feel a wholesome sorrow, wishing to be free.
Weary with saṃsāra, they should strive for liberation.
Forsaking thus this life's concerns,
They yearn to be enlightened in the next.
They should recoil from busy entertainment and distraction
And have but few defilements.
A broad and spacious mind they need
And attitudes of tolerance,
Of pure perception, and of great devotion.
They should be dedicated to the service of the Doctrine.
People such as this will gain the highest liberation.

2. They should greatly please their sublime teacher.
Through study and reflection and through meditation
They should train their minds.
In the quintessential pith instructions of the oral lineage
They should make a special effort,
And in long practice they should pass their days and nights.
Not straying to the ordinary even for an instant,
They should strive insistently
In what is most essential and profound.

3. Not transgressing the three vows
Belonging to the vehicles of śrāvakas,
Of bodhisattvas, and of vidyādharas,
Those who practice should rein in their minds
And seek as much as possible the benefit of others.
Turning all that manifests into the path of freedom.

4. Beginners in the practice
Must first accomplish their own benefit.
They should guard their minds in solitude,
Forsaking busy and distracting occupations.
They should rid themselves of adverse circumstances,
Taming their defilements through the use of antidotes.
Without confusing view and action,
They should give themselves to meditation.
Whichever of the five defilements
Comes to birth within their minds,
They should seize it mindfully
And use the antidote without distraction.
They should be careful, vigilant
And have a sense of shame and decency
In acts of body, speech, and mind.
Let them thereby discipline their minds.

5. Praise and blame, refusal and acceptance,
Pleasant and unpleasant—let them see all these as equal.
All, like magic shows and dreams, lack true existence.
They should think of them as all the same—
As just an echo's sound—and practice patience,
Examining the mind that clings to "I" and "self."
In brief, in all their actions let them not do anything
That contravenes the Dharma.
They should restrain their minds and do no harm to others.
Not indulging in defilement even for an instant,

Let them spend their days and nights in virtue.
This is of the highest moment.

6. Since in these present, evil times
People are uncouth and wild,
It is of great importance to secure
Your goal by practicing in solitude.
Unless the bird is fully fledged it cannot fly;
So too, unless you have clairvoyant knowledge,
No help can you provide for others.
Make efforts therefore to secure your goal,
And in your mind aspire to be of benefit to others.
Do not let your mind be lured by busy pastimes;
These are the deceitful tricks of Māra.
It is crucial to strive heartily in practice
So that in the hour of death
You will not be tormented by regret.

7. Now therefore inspect your mind!
Look! If now you were to die, how would you fare?
There's nothing sure in where you'll go
And what you will become.
By spending nights and days deceived in your distractions,
You meaninglessly waste your freedoms and advantages.
Meditate alone in solitude on the essential teachings.
Strive now to gain your ultimate objective.
Do you know where you will go at death?
Make effort therefore in this very instant.

8. Saṃsāra's false appearances
Are like a dangerous pathway filled with fear.
Remember! You must find a way to free yourself.
If once again you are beguiled,
You will forever wander in delusion.
Give rise to constancy therefore and keep it in your heart!

9. Now in your boat of freedoms and advantages
Traverse that ocean hard to cross:
Defilement and your clinging to a "self."
Thanks to the power of your merit,
Your one-in-a-hundred chance has dawned:
Your path to liberation and enlightenment!
So now, and with wholehearted constancy,
Secure your happiness and benefit!

10. Life is fleeting, every instant changing.
Distractions, wise in tricking you,
Postpone your virtuous deeds.
So strong is your old habit of delusion!
Defilements in their multitude
Befall you naturally and in an instant.
Whereas merit-bearing virtue hardly comes
However much you try!
So crucial is it then to strive
To turn back karma's powerful wind!

11. In saṃsāra, there is not the slightest joy.
Unbearable it is to think
Of all the sorrows in this wheel of life.
So now attend to methods that will set you free from it.
If instead of a sincere exertion
In the essence of the Doctrine,
You dawdle in a leisurely, infrequent practice,
No good will come of it.
So cultivate increasingly awareness of impermanence
Together with a wholesome sorrow with the world.
Gird yourself with effort in the practice.
Do not be distracted even for an instant.

12. If at the outset you have grasped this well,
You will in future swiftly come to the enlightened state.

And once your own good you have gained,
The good of others you will naturally achieve.
Now the supreme path you have discovered
Leading you to freedom from saṃsāra.
All that you do now accords with Dharma—
Thus you are the basis for attainment of enlightenment.

This completes the second vajra point of *Finding Rest in Meditation, a Teaching of the Great Perfection.*

3. THE THIRD VAJRA POINT

An Exposition of the Teachings to Be Practiced

---

1. The teaching to be practiced has three parts:
Preliminary, main part, and concluding section.

2. The preliminary teachings are set forth first.
The outer preliminaries are the understanding of
Impermanence and disenchantment with saṃsāra.
These uproot from deep within the mind
All clinging to this life.
The particular preliminaries are
Compassion and the attitude of bodhichitta whereby
All practice is transformed into the path of Mahāyāna.
Therefore, to begin with, train in these preliminaries.

3. The following preliminaries are far superior.
With all empowerments received,
You practice the two stages: generation [and perfection].
You perceive your body as a deity,
As deities the universe and beings.
Thus you overturn attachment to the real existence
Of what is commonly perceived.
Thanks to training in the deep path of the guru yoga,
Boundless blessings will arise
Through the powerful compassion of your teacher.
Obstacles are dissipated
And the two accomplishments attained.

So following the outer and particular preliminaries,
Meditate upon the two superior ones.

4. Through these four preliminaries,
Your mind embarks upon the unmistaken path.
And once you take this supreme path to freedom,
The fundamental nature swiftly manifests.
You will gain an easy skill in the main practice,
And there will be no obstacles.
Endless qualities you will possess:
Nearness to accomplishment and all the rest.
To train in the preliminaries is therefore most important.

5. Concerning the main practice,
Through the skillful means of concentration
On bliss, on luminosity, and on no-thought,
The fundamental nature of the mind
Will now be introduced to you.
Luminous primordial wisdom, free from all elaboration,
Uncontrived and coemergent, will arise.

6. First the introduction through the skillful method of great
   bliss.
Following the preliminary meditations previously explained,
Imagine that three channels, straight like pillars,
Pass through the center of the four chakras.
The channel on the right is white;
The channel on the left is red;
The central channel is blue and like a hollow tube,
The top of which lies in the Brahma aperture,
The lower end lies in the secret center.
In the central channel, at the level of the navel,
There is the letter A, whence fire blazes, causing the descent
Of nectar from the letter HANG located in the crown.
This fills up the four chakras and the space within the body.

When bliss pervades the body,
The nectar from the letter HANG
Flows down without a break
Upon the letter BAM located in the heart.
Meditate on this until the experience of bliss arises.
Then the letter BAM gets smaller and more fine.
Your mind now settles, free from thoughts and images,
In a state devoid of all conceptual construction.
Through this method, blissful concentration will arise,
And thus the state of calm abiding.

7. A state of mind then manifests
Beyond all thought, beyond expression,
A space-like state beyond the ordinary mind.
This is blissful, empty luminosity,
The state of Great Perfection—
Inconceivable and limpid dharmatā.

8. As you grow used to this,
Four experiences will come to you:
All that you perceive is easeful.
Day and night you do not leave the state of bliss.
Your mind is not disturbed by torments of desire and hate,
And wisdom manifests
Whereby the meaning of the Dharma's words is understood.

9. Through continued meditation,
The sun of qualities unbounded
Will arise within your mind:
Powers of vision, clairvoyant knowledge, and the rest.
This introduction to the nature of the mind
Through skillful means of great bliss
Is a crucial and profound instruction.

10. Second comes the introduction
Through the skillful means of luminosity.
First train in the preliminaries as before.
Then imagine the three channels
In such a way that *ro* and *kyang* have lower ends
That curve and penetrate the central channel
And upper ends that reach the nostril apertures.
As you thrice exhale stale air,
All illness, evil forces,
Sins, and obscurations are expelled.
And as you slowly inhale thrice,
The still world and its moving contents, melting into light,
Are drawn into the nostrils.
Passing thence through *ro* and *kyang*,
They penetrate the central channel
And then dissolve into a thumb-sized orb of light
Within the very center of your heart.
Concentrate on this as long as you are able.
Join the upper and the lower winds together.
As you exhale, retain a little air.
To inhale and to exhale gently is of great importance.
All the excellence moreover
Of the buddhas and exalted beings
Melts into your heart.
Do not wander from this state.
Through this method, there will manifest
A state of mind that's limpid, bright, and still.

11. Imagine that the radiance increases
From the light within your heart,
Which, setting the four chakras and your body all ablaze
And spilling outward, fills the world with light.
If thus you meditate both day and night,
Within a few days' time, your dreams will stop
And you will see these luminous appearances:

A moon, a blazing torch, fireflies, stars, and all the rest.
Outside and within, all will be pervaded by five-colored lights.
Because your mind is focused on the state of luminosity,
Calm abiding, śamatha, will manifest.

12. The light then gathers back into your heart
And slowly lessens in intensity until
Your mind rests in the state of emptiness.
Not focusing on anything,
Your mind rests in an empty, clear, and limpid state.
A luminosity by nature free from all elaboration manifests.

13. Such is primal wisdom,
Luminous and empty, uncontrived.
It is the fundamental mode of being
Of the Natural Great Perfection.

14. As you grow used to such a meditation,
Four experiences will manifest.
You will think that what appears
Is elusive, transparent, unimpeding.
Light will fill your days and nights.
Your clear and limpid mind will be unmoved by thought.
And free from the duality of grasper and the grasped,
Knowledge will come surging from within.

15. Through increased habituation,
Clairvoyant knowledge will arise.
You will develop powers of vision,
Perceiving extramental objects
Even when they are concealed by other things.
You will acquire the power of working miracles.
The introduction to the nature of the mind
By means of luminosity is the very essence
Of the most profound instructions.

16. Third, through the skillful means of no-thought
The nature of the mind is introduced.
Meditate, as previously, on the preliminaries.
Then implement the three points of the actual practice:
Propulsion, focusing, and then refinement.
The practice of propulsion is as follows:
Imagine that within your heart
Your mind rests, luminous by nature,
As a letter A or else a ball of light
The size of your own thumb.
Then forcefully reciting HA
One and twenty times,
Imagine that the letter is projected
Straight up through your crown,
Higher and higher into the sky above,
Until it's lost from sight.
Relax your mind and body deeply
And remain in meditative evenness.
The stream of thought
Will, in that instant, cease, and you will rest
Within a state that cannot be expressed in thought or word—
An experience beyond the reach of thought
In which there's nothing to be seen.

17. Now comes the stage of focusing awareness.
With your back turned to the sun,
Set your eyes upon the limpid sky.
Stay still and let your breath relax
Until its movement you no longer feel.
And from within the state of no-thought,
Freedom from elaboration will arise.
A meditative experience of space-like emptiness
Will come to birth.

18. Then undistracted, fix your gaze upon the sky,
And in the state of mental clarity,
Where thoughts do not develop or dissolve,
Meditate, considering that the earth and stones,
The hills and rocky crags,
The universe and beings in their entirety
Become the same as space, an unimpeded openness.
You have no apprehension
Even of your body as a gross, real form.
Settle in the state where space and your own mind
Are indistinguishable.
There is no recognition of an outer or an inner world
Or of something in between.
And in that state of space,
Relax deep down your body and your mind.
Memories and thoughts—all mental movement—
Come naturally to rest.
With no thoughts spreading and dissolving,
The mind stays in its natural state—
The ultimate condition of phenomena
And the mind beyond all thought and word
Are, at that time, not two.
A realization similar to space now dawns.
This is the essential nature of the Conquerors
Past, present, and to come.

19. As you meditate like this,
Four experiences occur.
All phenomena seem insubstantial
For you do not have a sense of gross materiality,
And day and night you do not leave the state of no-thought.
Since the five poisons naturally subside,
Your mind stream will be soft and gentle.
You will taste the spacious nature of all things.

20. Through training in this third technique of no-thought,
You will gain the powers of vision and clairvoyance,
Concentration, and various other qualities.
Through the union of skillful means and wisdom,
Calm abiding and deep insight,
You will gain for self and others
Immediate objectives and the final goal.

21. In the concluding explanations
Four topics are discussed:
Experiences in meditation,
Enhancement, realization, and the fruit.

22. Meditative experiences are of two kinds.
Those that have no flaw have been discussed above.
The faulty kind come from attachment and fixation
On bliss, on luminosity, and no-thought.
These consist in clinging to experiences
Of bliss, of luminosity, and of no-thought;
In considering such experiences
As objectives in themselves;
In fixating on them in a faulty manner;
And in mixing them with poison.
Erring bliss betokens common lust,
The loss of semen, and induces
Mostly discontent and dullness.
Erring luminosity implies the wild disturbance
Of the winds and common anger.
It leads mostly to the spreading forth
Of coarse and agitated thoughts.
Erring no-thought is a state of common ignorance,
Consisting mostly of a state of mental dullness,
Of sleepiness, of lethargy,
And a blank state in the mind.
When erring states

Or flawed experiences like these occur,
You must identify them
And with antidotes correct them.

23. For the sake of progress,
Use skillful means to counteract
Defective meditative experiences
And intensify your concentration.
There are three ways to correct
Such flawed experiences.
The best practitioners correct them
Through the application of the view:
All phenomena are mental imputations;
They are illusion-like and cannot be pinned down.
All of them, like space, are equal and beyond fixation.
From their own side, they are empty.
Confidently meditators settle in a state
In which they do not cling to anything.
Faulty and obscured experiences appear then
As the fundamental nature of the mind.
All hindrances are thus a spur to virtue;
All adversities are helpers to enlightenment.
On the ground of bliss, the mind is always happy,
And realization dawns like trackless space.

24. For practitioners of moderate strength,
Erring experiences are remedied through meditation.
They acquire a lucid clarity
By closely focusing their minds
And holding them with mindfulness.
They settle undistracted
In the state of bliss, of luminosity, and of no-thought.
Since distraction and the lack of focus
Are mistakes, it is important in one's meditation
Not to be distracted even for an instant.

25. When seed is being lost
Imagine in the vajra vase
The letter HUNG, from which a blazing fire
Burns all the semen that is in the body.
Meditate that none remains.
This will dispel the defect.
Apply this crucial point even when your seed
Is lost through illness or the action of an evil force.
Once you have destroyed all clinging to the bliss,
Meditate on bliss as empty.
Closely watch the mental state of ordinary lust,
And without tampering with it,
Remain within a state that's free from hope and fear.
In this way lust will naturally subside;
The blissful, empty, primal wisdom will arise.
The feeling of dejection is a fault
Arising from the weakened essence drop.
To counteract this, meditate upon
The blissful samādhi of blazing and of dripping.
Predominating dullness is a fault that comes
When the refined essential drops
Are not separated from those that have degenerated.
In this case, sit in upright posture;
Hold the vase breath; visualize a light that fills your heart
And the entire world. Then meditate on empty luminosity.
By this means, dullness is dispersed.

26. If you cling to luminosity,
This must be cleansed into a state that's free from all fixation.
If your mind is drowsy and unclear,
Meditate on it as bright and radiant.
If your mind is turbulent and agitated,
With eyes closed, meditate within your heart
Upon a light, a letter, lotus, sword, or else two vajras crossed.
These go down and down

As though fixed to a long, long rope,
Until they reach the golden ground,
The base of all the universe.
It is certainly impossible that this should fail
To dissipate all turbulence and agitation.
When ordinary anger and wild thoughts disturb,
Remain unmoved and they will all subside
In primal wisdom mirrorlike,
Luminous and empty.

27. When an erring experience of no-thought manifests,
Not clinging to it is the key point that will cleanse it.
When this ignorant state of mind is recognized
And directly watched, it instantly subsides.
The primal wisdom of the dharmadhātu manifests.
In the case of dullness, lethargy, or mental blank,
Visualize within your heart a light
That shoots out through the Brahma aperture
And stays, at a bow's length, suspended in the air.
As you concentrate on this,
Your mind is freed from all activity.
This is a crucial and profound instruction.

28. In general, it is crucial not to cling to anything.
If you are without hope or fear,
You are free from every obstacle.
Resting in the limpid state—
The luminous and empty nature of the mind—
Where no discursive thoughts proliferate,
Then surely you are free from dangerous paths
Of obstacles and flaws to be abandoned.

29. Practitioners of lowest power
Rectify their flawed experience
By the application of a threefold conduct:

Through ways of gazing, through material factors,
And through auspicious links.
The general way of gazing belongs
To the seven-point posture of Vairocana:
The legs are crossed, the gaze unmoving,
The breath is slow, the hands
Held in the meditation posture.
The neck is slightly bent,
The tongue's tip placed against the palate.
The eyes gaze down along the nose.
The wind-mind thus is held in balance,
And flawless meditative absorption,
Free from dullness and from agitation, manifests.
For every fault arises from disturbance
Of the channels, winds, and essence drops,
And these in turn arise through the disturbance
Of the key points of the body.
Therefore it is crucial to maintain them undisturbed
In meditative equipoise.
Since all good qualities arise
When channels, winds, and essence drops
Are undisturbed and functioning correctly,
It is essential that you understand
The body's vital points.

30. In yogic exercises
And the other trainings of the body,
A crucial point is to maintain
A state of unforced ease
Devoid of any agitation.
Another crucial point is that
The gentle way of holding breath
Will profit from the forceful one,
And conversely the forceful one will profit from the gentle.

To practice in accordance with your constitution
Is a matter of supreme importance.

31. In particular, when practicing on bliss,
The crucial point is that your arms be crossed
At the level of the elbows, and your eyes cast down,
While focusing your mind on bliss.
For practicing on luminosity,
Your hands should cover your knees;
Your breathing should be gentle,
And your eyes should stare directly into space.
The state of no-thought, on the other hand, is gained
From staying in the seven-point posture.

32. Material factors are
A place for practice suited to the time of year,
Companions, and your sustenance (both food and drink).
Adopt whichever helps experience.

33. Regarding the creation of auspicious links
When dealing with the loss of semen,
A thread of three strands spun by a young maiden
And empowered by mantra recitation
Should be tied around your waist.
This prevents emission of essential fluid.
When thoughts proliferate,
The state of no-thought is achieved
From swallowing a pill composed
Of sandal, cobra saffron, and "great fat."
In times of mental torpor, if you take
A pill composed of saffron, camphor, bodhichitta,
Concentration will be gained—the tantras say.

34. To enhance the unflawed states
Of bliss, of luminosity, of no-thought,

It is good to place your mind
On any object that is suitable.
Begin therefore by concentrating on an object,
And subsequently meditation will become
Spontaneously free of any reference.
This crucial point is most profound.
It is supreme and to be earnestly adopted by the fortunate.
To reject this method, dismissing it
As being endowed with characteristics,
Is indeed to take the path of fools.
Avoid this evil way of those who lack experience.

35. In particular, the best way to increase
The concentration upon bliss
Is, by drawing up the lower wind,
To pull the essence drops up from your secret center
And let them melt, dissolving in your crown.
Then settle in a state devoid of reference.
Subsequently join the lower and the upper winds
And hold the vase breath.
Focusing your mind upon your heart,
Remain within the unborn nature.
You rest thus in a state of bliss and luminosity
That's free from mind's proliferation.

36. From time to time perform
The "vigorous shaking of the lion."
Draw down, reverse, draw up, and spread
The essence drops
And confidently settle in the nature of the mind.
Implement the crucial aspects
Of this yogic exercise
As you have seen them shown
According to your lineage.

37. For drawing down the essence drops,
Perform the mudrā of embracing
And, sitting straight, exert
A downward pressure on your lower parts.
Visualize that bodhichitta
Is made to flow down from the HANG.
And when it falls into your secret center,
Focus on the ensuing bliss.

38. Then reverse the flow and draw it upward.
Hold your fists at the level of your kidneys
And "join the ocean and the rock."
Draw up the lower wind
And touch your tongue-tip to your palate.
Rolling up your eyes, push down and shake your head.
Imagine that the essence drops—
As though strung on a silken thread—
Melt one into the next,
Till the crown of the head is reached.

39. For the spreading of the essence drops,
Act as you would draw a bowstring
And strongly agitate your arms and legs.
Then with your tongue-tip placed against your teeth,
Pronouncing si, hiss out your breath.

40. Rest now with conviction in the nature of the mind.
Lie down upon your back
With gentle breath, your mind at ease.
Do not think of anything; do not grasp at anything—
Rest in the nature free from mental movement.
By this means, great bliss, enlightenment
Will be accomplished without hindrance.

41. The best way to enhance
Your concentration upon luminosity
Is by means of breathing.
The gentle and the forceful ways
By which the breath is held
Enhance each other.
In particular it is crucial to combine in alternation
The slow and gentle holding of the breath
Both outside and within.
It has been taught that one should train in many other ways
Concerning numbers, colors, touch, and so forth.
But here, through unique instruction,
All will be accomplished.
This training is indeed the sovereign method.

42. Applying all the key points of the body
As was previously explained,
Especially that of an unmoving gaze,
Breathe evenly and very slowly
Through your mouth and both your nostrils.
Relax completely in the "ordinary,"
That is, the natural, state of openness and freedom.
The key point of the mind is not to focus
Upon anything, but to leave it naturally as it is.
Lie down on your back and stretch your arms and legs.
Then shouting HA, fix your mind upon the sky.
Rest calmly then, without distraction,
Free from thought's proliferation and dissolution.
The wind-mind rests then in the blissful state
Of natural openness and freedom.
This is the door through which arise
All perfect qualities countless and unhindered.

43. Your body then feels light.
No breath is felt.

All movement of the mind is stilled.
The mind is luminous and clear
And there occurs clairvoyant knowledge.
Swift-footedness is gained;
Your skin will gleam and shine;
And concentration will arise.
Signs there will be indicating
That the wind-mind has now gone
Into the central channel.
This is a supreme instruction.
It is extremely secret, most profound.

44. To enhance your concentration
On the state of no-thought similar to space,
Deeply let your mind and body rest
And focus on an object single-pointedly.
As you fix strongly on this object
Free from all distraction,
All other thoughts subside
Within this one experience of this object.
Then even the idea of this object vanishes completely.
The appearance of the thing remains,
And yet there is no grasping onto it—
It arises, yet is empty.

45. This is a crucial point, and in addition,
You must train as follows.
Focusing from time to time on some external object,
Expel your breath and hold it outside
For as long as you can manage.
The state of no-thought will arise.
Sometimes hold your breath within
And stay unwavering and undistracted,
Focused on an object in your body—
Whether in the upper or the lower part.

Sometimes leave your mind
Just as it is, without support,
Remaining in a state in which,
Though things appear, you do not cling to them.
On the basis of this crucial explanation,
The wisdom of the dharmakāya, free from thoughts,
Will, from within, arise all by itself.

46. The general way of heightening the concentrations
On bliss, on luminosity, and on no-thought
Rests in the accumulations both of wisdom and of merit,
The cleansing of all obscurations,
The practice of the generation and perfection stages,
And the most highly praised profound path of the guru yoga.
This instruction is supreme and ultimate.
The fortunate who wish for liberation
Should earnestly embrace it.

47. The realizations that arise through meditating thus
Are all of the same taste.
They are not manifold; they are not different.
It is like those who come from three directions
And meet together in a single place,
And like the different flowing streams
That join and are as one within a single sea.
Bliss, luminosity, and no-thought—
Whichever of these methods one may practice—
When mental movement comes to complete rest
And in the nature of the mind, the unborn space, dissolves,
The enlightened mind, devoid of concepts
(Whether of existence or of nonexistence),
The sun of fundamental nature, bright and clear,
Will rise up from within.
In this realization, changeless and unmoving,
There is nothing to be added, nothing to remove.

It is by its nature the sugatagarbha
Commensurate with space itself.

48. At that moment, in the ocean of samādhi—
Calm abiding and deep insight,
One-pointed, clear, immaculate—
Phenomena are like reflections,
Free of all intrinsic being,
Mirrored without partiality or clinging.
Their nature has been realized as
Appearances and emptiness in union.
Appearances are empty;
They resemble magical illusions.
They cannot be pinned down.
The vast expanse of realization
Of this union indivisible,
The luminosity that rises from within,
Is brought forth through this pith instruction.

49. It is through the teacher's blessing that you see
The self-arisen primal wisdom, inexpressible,
Beyond both word and thought.
And in the moment of its seeing,
Timeless are the three times,
No difference separates the future from the past.
This is the Wisdom That Has Gone Beyond; the Middle Way;
The Stilling (of all thought and sorrow); the Great Seal;
The Great Perfection of the quintessential ultimate reality,
That is, the fundamental natural state
Where, from the very first,
Phenomena are all exhausted.
It is mind's luminosity,
The self-arisen primal wisdom.
Many names it has received, yet all have but one meaning:
Ultimate reality, beyond the range

Of speech, of thought, of explanation:
The enlightened mind,
The space-like nature where saṃsāra and nirvāṇa are not two.

50. Unconfined, beyond all partiality,
Not trammeled in the snare of tenets,
Free from the discursive mind,
Nondual, perfect, great equality,
The wisdom of the Conquerors,
The vast expanse beyond extremes.
This is what practitioners should fully recognize.

51. The varying results of all these concentrations,
Fully mastered, are as follows.
In the immediate term, through union
Of bliss, of luminosity, and no-thought,
Countless qualities—clairvoyant knowledge,
Powers of vision—all are gained.
And on the final level,
The enlightened wish-fulfilling qualities
Of the three kāyas are accomplished.
The twofold purpose for oneself and others
Is spontaneously achieved.

This completes the third vajra point of *Finding Rest in Meditation*,
a Teaching of the Great Perfection.

CONCLUDING VERSES

1. Through the merit of explaining
This quintessential teaching
Deep and vast,
A way of practice that will lead to peace,
May every being reach enlightenment
Adorned with two sublime accumulations,
Enjoying endless riches of enlightened deeds
Whereby to satisfy all wishes.

2. As a distillation of the essence
Of the crucial points of his own practice,
Drimé Özer, child of the Victorious Ones,
For the sake of those to come,
Has well set down this lucid explanation
On the slopes of Gangri Thökar.

3. You who wish for liberation,
Be diligent in following my words.
For thus you will perfect the two objectives
According to immediate need and for the final goal,
And swiftly gain contentment
In the island of great bliss.

This concludes the treatise *Finding Rest in Meditation, a Teaching of the Great Perfection.*

PART TWO

THE CHARIOT OF
SURPASSING PURITY

*Longchenpa's Autocommentary on
Finding Rest in Meditation*

IN SANSKRIT
Mahāsandhidhyānaviśrāntasayavrittirathaviśuddhakanāma

IN TIBETAN
*rDzogs pa chen po bsam gtan ngal gso'i 'grel pa
shing rta rnam dag ces bya ba*

PROLOGUE

Homage to you, O glorious Samantabhadra!

Your nature is the ultimate expanse,
Primordial and perfect peace.
Though free of all conceptual constructs,
It is yet embellished by the kāyas and the wisdoms
Present of themselves.
From this there radiates a myriad rays of light
Performing every kind of action
In the field of those who might be trained.
In joy and veneration I bow down to you
Samantabhadra, sun of love and knowledge—
To you and all the buddhas and their bodhisattva heirs.

Among the teachings of the Natural Great Perfection,[14]
Whose path brings beings blessed with perfect fortune
To the city of their freedom,
Here I shall set forth this commentary,
The Chariot of Surpassing Purity.

The peak and summit of all the infinite discourses of the Sugata is
the class of teachings belonging to the Natural Great Perfection.
The stages in which an individual person may put this teaching
into practice are defined in my text *Finding Rest in Meditation*. In
the present commentary, I shall clearly describe the key points of
its pith instructions.

The text begins with an expression of homage.

> Primordial nature,
> Pure and vast expanse like space itself,
> Supreme reality, unmoving,
> Utterly devoid of all elaboration,
> Clear and lucent nature of the mind itself,
> The essence of enlightenment—
> In seeing this unmoving and unchanging perfect ground,
> I bow in homage.

The ground of the Great Perfection is the nature of the mind, self-arisen primordial wisdom, which is motionless and transcends all conceptual extremes. Its nature is beyond differentiation. It is empty like an all-accommodating space and is luminous like the unclouded sun and moon. Like a jewel, it is in itself replete with excellence. It is within this ground, or rather this ultimate expanse—which while not existing in any way, may manifest as anything at all—that saṃsāra and nirvāṇa both subsist. And through recognizing this unmoving and unchanging ground, awareness itself, I pay homage to it. As it is said in the *All-Creating King Tantra*,

> *Kyé!* Teacher of the Teachers, all-creating King!
> Expanse of ultimate reality,
> Nature of the buddhas of the triple time,
> You do not spurn saṃsāra,
> Your compassion takes no sides,
> To you, O Teacher, all-creating King, I bow!

And it is also said in the *Dohā*, the songs of realization,

> The nature of the mind is the sole seed of everything.
> Existence and nirvāṇa both emerge from it.
> I bow down to this mind that like a wish-fulfilling gem
> Is giver of the fruits one may desire.

And again in the *Ratnāvalī* we find,

> Like water into water merging,
> Butter into butter mixing,
> Well-seeing primal wisdom self-cognizing—
> 'Tis thus that I bow down to it.

Then comes the promise to compose the text of the commentary.

> **That the surpassing wonder of the Conqueror's mind**
> **Be realized—primal wisdom, self-cognizing—**
> **I distilled the essence of the tantras, commentaries, and**
> **pith instructions.**
> **Pay heed! I shall explain them in the light of my experience.**

The subject of these pith instructions is self-cognizing primordial wisdom. This wisdom is the mother of all the buddhas, past, present, and to come. I will therefore explain it for the sake of future generations according to how I myself have practiced it. It is said in the *Abridged Prajñāpāramitā-sūtra*,

> The path of past and future Conquerors
> Residing in the ten directions
> Is this transcendent virtue, nothing else.

The very same point is made in the *Praise to the Mother*,

> No name, no thought, no explanation is there
> For the Wisdom That Has Gone Beyond.
> Unceasing and unborn, the very character of space,
> It is the sphere of self-cognizing wisdom.
> I bow to this, the mother of Victorious Ones
> Past, present, and to come.

What is the relevance of citing this transcendent virtue in the context of an exposition of the Great Perfection? The reason is that transcendent wisdom itself *is* the Great Perfection.[15] For this is how all the Victorious Ones of the three times refer to awareness itself. It is that from which they take their birth. As it is said in the *All-Creating King,*

> *Kyé!* I am the essence uncontrived just as it is.
> I am beyond both being and nonbeing.
> The Victorious Ones of the three times come forth from me,
> Thus truly am I called the mother of Victorious Ones.

This section reveals the reason for the composition of this treatise. I shall now explain the main body of the root text first briefly and then in detail.

First, there comes a brief and summary description of its pith instructions.

> **On mountain peaks and lake isles, or in forest groves,**
> **Congenial to the mind in the four seasons of the year,**
> **With single-pointed concentration, serene, unmoving,**
> **Meditate on luminosity devoid of mind's construction.**
> **Depending on three things is this accomplished:**
> **The place, the persons, and the practices they implement.**

If those who wish for liberation settle evenly in profound concentration in places suited to their temperament and appropriate to the four seasons of the year, it is certain that they will achieve their purpose. And since liberation is perfectly accomplished thanks to three factors—the place where the practice is pursued, the practitioners themselves, and the teachings they practice—these three points form the adamantine body of this treatise, and I shall now explain them successively and in detail.

The First Vajra Point

Concerning the Place of Practice

There are different locations appropriate to the four seasons of the year.

1. First, the place we shall consider.
This should be a pleasant solitude
Amenable for practice in the year's four seasons.
In summer you should meditate
In regions that are cool and in cool habitations,
In snowy places, mountaintops,
In shelters made of bamboo, reeds, or grass.
In autumn you should stay in regions and in dwellings
   where
The cold and heat are of an equal strength,
In places such as woodlands, hillsides, rocky forts,
With corresponding conduct, food, and clothing.
In wintertime, you should adapt your bedding, food, and
   dress
And live in dwellings that are warm and in low-lying
   regions:
Forests, caverns, houses made of earth.
In spring it's most important to retire
To mountains, forests, islands, and to dwell in shelters
Where the heat and cold are balanced,
With food and dress and conduct all in harmony.

This is all described in a text composed by the great master Garab Dorje, the *Profound Practice of Yoga in the Four Seasons*. In summertime when fire predominates, the outer and inner elements are hot, and one should therefore keep to places that are cool, adopting appropriate conduct in terms of cooling food and light clothing. Autumn is the season of wind. It is the time when the outer and inner elements come to ripeness. One should therefore stay in open, airy places and adjust one's conduct, food, and clothing accordingly. Winter is the time when water predominates. The outer and inner elements are cool, and therefore one's dwelling place, dress, food, and so on should be warm. Finally, the spring is the time of earth. The outer and inner elements are on the verge of growth. It is therefore important to be in places, and to adopt a diet and a way of dressing, in which cold and heat are evenly balanced. For the cycle of dependent arising has two aspects: outer and inner. As it is said in the *Kālacakra Tantra*, "As without, so within."

The characteristics of various dwelling places are now discussed together with the practices for which they are propitious.

2. The external and internal cycles of dependence coincide.
Therefore, stay in pleasant solitudes, in places of delight.
Since on mountain heights the mind is clear and vast,
These regions, where all mental dullness clarifies,
Are beneficial to the practice of the generation stage.
In snowy lands, the mind is bright
With lucid concentration.
These places are propitious for the practice of deep insight,
For here there are few obstacles.
In forest groves, the mind grows calm
And mental stillness manifests.
These are places where one trains in calm abiding
And where mental bliss grows strong.
At the foot of rocky crags, a sense of transience
And a weary sorrow with saṃsāra strengthens.
The clear and powerful union

Of calm abiding and deep insight is achieved.
On riverbanks, the mind's imagination is curtailed.
Sorrow at saṃsāra and the decisive wish
To part from it will rapidly develop.
Charnel grounds are powerful places
Where accomplishment is swift.
Such places, it is taught, are most propitious
For any of the practices of generation and perfection.

When meditators—be they beginners, practitioners of moderate proficiency, or perfectly accomplished yogis—live in such places, knowing how to conduct themselves in retreat as it has been explained, the view and meditation particular to each of them will grow and will be attained. For the excellent qualities of these locations will become friends and helpers in the accomplishment of their paths.

Locations suited to the meditative proficiency of practitioners are now described.

3. In towns and markets, empty houses, lonely trees,
Where human beings congregate or elves and spirits pass,
Beginners are distracted and are hindered in their practice.
For those who have stability,
Such places are propitious and supremely praised.
Lonely temples, offering shrines,
Where *gyalgong* spirits dwell, are places where
The mind does not find rest
And many thoughts of enmity arise.
In places such as caverns in the earth,
Which are abodes of *senmo* hags,
Desire arises and an extreme dullness or an
 agitation of the mind.
Lonely trees are haunts of *mamos* and of ḍākinīs;
Cliffs and promontories are lairs
Of *theurang* wights and wild, ferocious *tsen*.

> All such places, it is said, provoke wild agitation
> In the mind and many obstacles.
> In haunts of outcasts, nāgas, *nyen* wraiths, spirits of the
>   place,
> On lakeside, grassy heath, in woodland wilds,
> In valleys strewn with healing herbs,
> Adorned with flowers and fruit and berry-bearing trees,
> All pleasing to the mind, at first one is content,
> But later many obstacles befall.

Places that are the haunts of evil worldly gods and spirits are suited to the practice of yogis who are strong and stable in their meditation. They are not good, however, for the meditation, or as the regular habitat, of beginners in the practice, who should consequently avoid them. On the other hand, the neighborhood of mountain gods, of nāgas, *tsen* and *menmo* spirits, and other nonhuman entities who take pleasure in virtue are always good places in which to stay. For such beings give their protection; they encourage favorable circumstances and prevent the arising of adversity.

The place of practice should be carefully checked.

> 4. In brief, in those localities and dwellings
> That at first seem pleasant but with familiarity
> Lose their charm, only slight accomplishment is gained.
> But places that at first seem fearful and forbidding
> Yet turn to good as you grow used to them
> Are of great power, and great accomplishment is swift to
>   come,
> While obstacles do not occur.
> All other places, being neutral, neither benefit nor harm.

These are important key points. If one examines different locations for two weeks, their qualities can be assessed with certainty. Therefore,

> 5. Since in dependence on your dwelling place
> Your inner mind is changed, and virtuous practice
> Thrives or languishes, to ponder thus your dwelling
> Is a point, so it is said, of high importance.

As it is said in the *Gradual Path of Secret Mantra*, "Dwelling places have a twofold character: either they foster an increase in virtue or they do not."

Dwelling places are then briefly described in relation to the four activities.

> 6. There are, in sum, four kinds of dwelling place
> According to the four activities.
> In places suitable for pacifying, the mind is focused
>   naturally.
> Places suitable for increase are delightful,
> Filled with splendor and magnificence.
> Places that are ravishing and stimulate attachment
> Are suited to the action of attracting.
> Places suited to the fierce activity
> Provoke anxiety and panic-fear.
> There are in fact unnumbered subdivisions of such places.
> But here, as aids to concentration,
> Places suitable for pacifying are the best.
> The others, here, are not considered
> For fear of great prolixity.

Every place in the outer environment is propitious to one or other of the four activities. In places that are appropriate for the activity of pacification, the mind is naturally inclined to calm, and the meditative concentration of no-thought arises of its own accord. By contrast, places suitable for the activity of increase are magnificent and thrill the mind with joyful excitation. Places suited to the activity of magnetizing or attracting stimulate attachment, while the kinds of places appropriate to ferocious activity inspire one with feelings of anxiety and fear. The physical configurations of these places are, respectively, round, square, semicircular, and triangular; their predominant colors are white, yellow, red, and dark green. Moreover, if each kind of place is again subdivided fourfold (peaceful-peaceful, peaceful-increasing, peaceful-attracting, and so on), we arrive at sixteen subdivisions. And each of these can be further classified indefinitely. But enough of such complexity! In the present context, the instruction is given for living in a peaceful kind of dwelling place, propitious to the growth of meditative concentration.

A meditation shelter in a peaceful environment is now described.

> 7. A meditation shelter in a peaceful place
> Should be set apart in solitude, in a site that is congenial.
> A very open, spacious place where all around
> One sees the sky is most conducive.

A meditation shelter set in a position that is open and commands a wide and distant view is conducive to the natural arising of meditative concentration. Hindrances will be rare in such locations.

Next comes a description of places suitable for the different daytime and nighttime practices.

> 8. The dark house for the nighttime yoga
> Has two sets of walls.
> In the center of an inner, elevated room,
> Your headrest should be in the north,
> As when the Buddha passed into nirvāṇa.
> For the daytime yoga in the light,
> The hermitage should have a vast expanse in front
> With open sky and distant views
> Of snowy mountains, falling water,
> Woods, and valleys.
> In such a place the mind is clear and limpid,
> And heat and cold should be in equilibrium.

In preparation for the nighttime practice, one should build a dark hermitage equipped with two sets of walls. Some people say that the hermitage should be round like the circle of the sun, but this is very inconvenient for walking and sitting. Therefore, around a central point, a hermitage should be constructed with a double wall and with openings for light on the eastern, southern, and western sides. The [concentric] walls should be at one full arm span from the central point for the first wall, and then at one full arm span plus an arrow's length for the second wall. The door of the inner meditation room [located within the inner wall] should be in the westerly direction. The door of the inner wall itself should face the south, and the door of the outer wall should face east. A window should be made in each of the walls in the four directions so as to illuminate the inner room [when one is not in session] and provide light for the practice of circumambulation and so on. When one is in the meditation room during practice sessions, however, the windows should be blocked and one should meditate facing the opening in the northern wall.[16]

The place for the daytime yoga should be on the roof of the hermitage, beneath a half-shelter facing south. If one practices in such an open area, where one can see far into the distance, one's meditative concentration will be very clear.

The place for the common practice of calm abiding is now described.

> 9. For the practice of abiding in tranquility,
> A hermitage enclosed is most propitious
> For the natural rising of the state of mental calm.
> When practicing deep insight,
> A spacious place that has a vast and open view
> Is most important.
> It should always be a pleasant place
> Appropriate to the season.

In one of the four directions on the outside of the hermitage, there should be an open area, a spacious meadow fenced in by a brake of undergrowth reaching to one's waist. In places like this, the state of calm abiding arises of its own accord. Then if one sits on a small seat in an elevated position, so that one has a wide-ranging view, deep insight naturally arises.

What then are the regions where calm abiding and deep insight can arise?

> 10. Low-lying, darksome places such as forests and ravines
> Are places fit for calm abiding.
> High lands, such as snowy mountains,
> Are the places for deep insight.
> It is important thus to know these differences.

In places like forests and ravines amid the mountain crags, the mind withdraws within, and therefore such locations are appropriate for the practice of calm abiding. In high places, on the other hand, the mind becomes lucid and spacious. It is important to understand that such places are beneficial for the practice of deep insight.

Concluding advice now follows about the places that are to be sought or avoided.

> 11. In brief, the places and the hermitages
> Where you feel a sadness for saṃsāra
> And the wish to free yourself,
> Locations where your mind, reined in,
> Rests in the present and your concentration grows—
> These are sites connecting you to virtue.
> You should live in such environments
> Resembling the place of Buddha's own enlightenment.
> Places where your virtue lessens and defilement grows,
> Where you fall beneath the influence
> Of the distracting busyness of life,
> Are demonic dens of evil deeds avoided by the wise.

Padma, self-arisen, has explained them thus,
And those who wish for freedom should take heed.

Places and dwellings that are conducive to the growth of virtue,
where faith and a strong determination to leave saṃsāra develop,
resemble the very place where the Buddha gained enlightenment.
These are the kinds of place where one should live. By contrast,
environments where conflict and defilement spread, where the distractions and the busy activities of this present life increase, should
be recognized and abandoned for what they are: devilish regions
fit for evil deeds. In his pith instructions called the *Garland of the
Fortress of Views*,[17] the great master Padmasambhava spoke about
the importance of the place in which the Dharma is practiced. No
better situation can be found than places where virtue and concentration increase. He therefore advised us to live in such places and
said that we should take steps to shun areas marked by an increase
of conflict and negativity since they are obstacles on the path of
liberation.

In peaceful places may I be sustained
By pure water and the glory of austerity.
Abandoning distraction and life's busy entertainments,
May I deeply concentrate and meditate on ultimate reality.

May I shun the birthplace of a host of sorrows,
The fences of the city of saṃsāra,
And gain the peace of liberation,
The place of high enlightenment,
Nirvāṇa's blissful garden paradise.

A man like me, these days, can do no good to beings.
In these evil times, therefore, I will forsake
Society and worldly things.
Abandoning the deeds and dissipations of this life,
May I open wide the four doors of the precious hidden land.

———————

This completes the first vajra point of *The Chariot of Surpassing Purity*, a commentary on *Finding Rest in Meditation, a Teaching of the Great Perfection.*

THE SECOND VAJRA POINT
Concerning Those Who Practice Meditation

I shall now explain the characteristics of meditators who practice in retreat.

> 1. Now persons who engage in practice
> Should have diligence and faith
> And feel a wholesome sorrow, wishing to be free.
> Weary with saṃsāra, they should strive for liberation.
> Forsaking thus this life's concerns,
> They yearn to be enlightened in the next.
> They should recoil from busy entertainment and distraction
> And have but few defilements.
> A broad and spacious mind they need
> And attitudes of tolerance,
> Of pure perception, and of great devotion.
> They should be dedicated to the service of the Doctrine.
> People such as this will gain the highest liberation.

Faith, diligence, and the determined wish to free oneself from saṃsāra are like the indispensable soil in which the Dharma grows. Weariness with saṃsāra is the entrance to the Dharma, the necessary requisite for pursuing the path to liberation. Striving for the bliss of nirvāṇa is like the seed of enlightenment. To turn away from and to forsake the concerns of this life are the means to achieving liberation from saṃsāra. The wish for definitive enlightenment is—of the three conditions necessary for the growth of a seed—like water and manure. To withdraw from busy activities and defilement is itself to practice an instruction whereby all adverse circumstances are naturally removed. To have an attitude of pure perception and devotion is the natural cause and condition for the increase of one's harvest of virtue. A stable temperament that respects and serves the teachings will quickly bring to ripeness the fruits of the path of liberation. Those who have such characteristics should be known as supreme vessels.

The *All-Creating King*, moreover, has this to say,

> Those with faith, samaya, and great diligence,
> Who have compassion, joy, and sorrow with saṃsāra
> And are possessed of stable temperaments;
> Those who have no clinging to their bodies,
> To their children, spouses, servants, and attendants,
> And offer them with faith and joy—
> Such people have the seal of faith and of samaya.
> To them the quintessential teaching should be given.

It is at this point also that this same text speaks of vessels that are to be rejected.

> Wrong persons, those who are not proper vessels,
> Are now shown.
> They are attached to fame and worldly things.
> They are puffed up with pride
> And have no reverence for holy beings.
> Their minds are fickle, without constancy.
> All is show. For substances of practice they have no regard.
> From guessed-at meditation they expect immediate results.
> The many teachings that they know are seen awry.
> They falsely praise themselves and others they defame,
> And cultivate malevolence.
> To all such people do not give the teachings;
> Keep them perfectly concealed.

Those who are perfect vessels should practice in the following way.

2. They should greatly please their sublime teacher.
Through study and reflection and through meditation
They should train their minds.
In the quintessential pith instructions of the oral lineage
They should make a special effort,
And in long practice they should pass their days and nights.
Not straying to the ordinary even for an instant,
They should strive insistently
In what is most essential and profound.

Since it is the sublime teacher who gives access to the door of liberation, those who wish to gain accomplishment should give him pleasing service. And in harmony with their learning, reflection, and meditation, they should be diligent and undistracted in the essential practice. The tantra entitled *Glorious Exhaustion of the Four Elements* declares,

Faithful ones who wish to gain accomplishment!
Accomplishment derives from pleasing service to the
teacher.
And so with all that you possess,
Strive perfectly in making offerings to your teacher.

The foundation for the path to liberation is laid in the following way.

3. Not transgressing the three vows
Belonging to the vehicles of śrāvakas,
Of bodhisattvas, and of vidyādharas,
Those who practice should rein in their minds
And seek as much as possible the benefit of others,
Turning all that manifests into the path of freedom.

In whichever practice one may be engaged, it is necessary to train in the disciplines associated with the three vows. If one wishes for the enlightenment of the śrāvakas, it is necessary to keep the vows of individual liberation, or prātimokṣa. If one wishes for unsurpassed enlightenment after three immeasurable kalpas[18] or more, one must train in the bodhisattva vows. If one wishes to gain enlightenment swiftly—in the space of one or several lives—one must abide by the vows of the Secret Mantra. Since the [lower] sets of vows are gradually and qualitatively enhanced [by those that follow] while remaining distinct in terms of their nominal aspects, these three distinct disciplines are said to be the foundation [of all qualities]. As Nāgārjuna has said,

> The Buddha said that, as the earth
> Is ground and basis for everything and all that lives,
> Likewise discipline
> Is ground and basis of all qualities.

In general, for all practices oriented toward the freedom of enlightenment, one must receive the vows. For positive actions undertaken outside the framework of the vows constitute a neutral kind of virtue that is unable to take one beyond saṃsāra. If, however, one practices perfectly and without making mistakes on the path of the vows of individual liberation, one will gain the enlightenment of the śrāvakas and will cease to wander in saṃsāra. Then, with the help of the bodhisattva vows, one will achieve enlightenment after three immeasurable kalpas. Finally, through the vows of the Secret Mantra one may gain enlightenment within the space of a single life. For those who have the three kinds of vows, there is the possibility of downfalls or violations of the precepts. For those without vows, there are no downfalls, but neither are there any merits. For if there is no field, there is neither an autumn harvest nor the possibility of its being destroyed by frost and hail.

The three vows should be understood in the following way. The vows of individual liberation consist in restraints placed on the mind so that it is not polluted by defilement and nonvirtue. The bodhisattva vows consist in securing the benefit of others through consistently positive action. The vidyādhara vows of the Secret Mantra consist in spontaneously accomplishing the twofold goal by visualizing beings, oneself and others, as deities and their dwelling places as immeasurable palaces, and by utilizing sense pleasures as the path. Concerning the conduct related to the three vows, this consists, in the case of the vows of individual liberation, in turning away from the infliction of harm and from the defilements that are the cause of this. In the case of the bodhisattva vows, it consists in securing the welfare of others. Finally, in the case of the vows of the Secret Mantra, it consists in not parting from the single maṇḍala of purity and equality.[19]

Regarding the way in which the three vows are observed by an individual person, it is said by some that until one embarks on the [Mahāyāna] path, one keeps the vows of individual liberation. Subsequently, and until one reaches the level of "warmth" on the path of joining,[20] the bodhisattva vows are observed. It is only from this point onward that the vows of the Secret Mantra are observed. This assertion is unacceptable, for practitioners of the Vajrayāna meditate on the path, observing all three kinds of vows, from the very beginning. This mistaken position is refuted by the following citation:

> Those who are the best practitioners
> Must have all the vows and perfectly observe them.

Others are of the opinion that the vows are observed in transmuted form. For example, when copper ore is smelted, copper is produced. If tin is added to the copper, brass is produced. If lead is subsequently added, the alloy turns into bronze. In the same way, when a higher vow is received, the lower one is transmuted, with the result that it is sufficient to observe only the mantra vows. This too is incorrect and is invalidated by the *Sacred Primordial Buddha Tantra*, where it is explained that "To disregard [a vow] is a misdeed by its very nature." This means that to overlook the lower vows is a downfall. All the vows are to be observed.

Still others believe that [when one kind of vow is being observed] the others are as if dormant or eclipsed. This, however, is irrelevant, because whether the higher vow or a lower vow is eclipsed, all vows retain their individual character.

The view that the three vows are of the same substance and aspect is not tenable either. They are not identical in substance, aspect, or time, because of the following three factors. First, they do not originate from the same causes; second, they are contradictory; and finally, they are not coterminous.

The belief that a lower vow is relinquished when a higher vow is received is also unacceptable, for such an explanation is nowhere found.

What then is the truth of the matter? There are six principles according to which the three vows are observed all together by a single individual. First, the aspects of the three vows remain distinct. Second, the vows are the same in purpose as preventives or remedies. Third, the nature of the vows is transmuted. Fourth, the three vows are gradually and qualitatively enhanced. Fifth, there is no essential contradiction between them. And sixth, their observance should chiefly be appropriate to the moment.[21]

According to the first principle, when it is said that the aspects of the vows remain distinct, the meaning is that they retain their own particular character.[22]

The second principle states that the three vows are all the same in serving the same purpose and acting as preventives [of unwholesome actions].[23] It is as the saying goes, "Let everyone get up and build the fort."[24] The three vows are all the same in that they all hold back negativity from the mind stream. As it is said in the Vinaya texts,

> You should understand that any teaching that, whether
> directly or indirectly, becomes a cause of attachment
> and is not the cause of the relinquishment of attachment

is not virtuous. It is not the Vinaya; it is not the doctrine of our Teacher. You should understand that any teaching that, whether directly or indirectly, becomes a cause of the relinquishment of attachment and is not the cause of attachment is virtuous. It is the Vinaya; it is the doctrine of our Teacher.

The text continues at length regarding anger and each of the other defilements.

In this respect, a monk of chaste and celibate life and a yogi who takes up the path of the third empowerment are fundamentally the same in the sense that, whereas the monk, while having the capacity to do so, does not engage in sexual activity and is not stained by lust, the yogi, who does engage in sexual activity, is also unstained by lust. Therefore, in relation to the impurity of desire, the vows of both are perfectly the same in the essential article of purpose and remedial quality. If, in all situations, the principal factor were simply nonindulgence in sexual activity, it would be correct to say that eunuchs and little children were capable of observing the vow [of pure conduct].

Moreover, if the vows of individual liberation and those associated with the third empowerment were in direct contradiction, it would follow that the only appropriate supports for the Secret Mantra would be laypeople. However, the root tantra of the *Kālacakra* says that "Among the three kinds of practitioner, the monk is best." And the *Saṃvarodaya* says, "O nobly born, have you in the past sincerely taken monastic ordination according to the Vinaya (an ordination that is said to be the excellent basis for all good qualities)? Have you lived according to the vows of individual liberation? Have you taken refuge in the Three Jewels? Or do you aspire to do so?"

The *Two-Part Hevajra Tantra* says,

The vows of all the buddhas
Utterly abide in *Ēwam*.

Éwam is the perfect bliss,
Which thanks to the empowerment is correctly known.

And,

Those who have been burned in lustful fires
Will be freed by lust itself.

And the *Mañjuśrī Tantra* says,

Worldly attachment is eliminated
By joyful attachment to emptiness.

In short, the elimination of defilement through the vows of individual liberation, the purification of defilement by means of the bodhisattva vows, and the adoption of defilement as the path by the Secret Mantra are all the same in that they eliminate actual defilement. Respectively, this is like purging a poison, using it as a medicine, or consuming it after a mantra has been applied to it. The three cases are the same in that they all eliminate the noxious effect of the poison and achieve the same objective of escaping death. If the downfalls are thus assessed with regard to the three vows, it is in accordance with the vows of individual liberation that one should keep oneself from downfalls related to nonvirtue and wrongdoing. In accordance with the higher vows, one must also protect oneself from those downfalls that are not motivated by selfish attachment. Finally, one should strenuously guard against all that is prohibited by worldly custom and by the vows themselves that leads others to lose faith.

The conduct of a Vajrayāna monk must be free from misdeeds and must be appropriate to a given situation. Until he gains genuine experience [of blissful and empty primordial wisdom], he must principally observe the common vows. When he gains this experience, however, there will be a difference in his outer and inner way of behaving. At the time of secret activities, and on the four occasions when he and others receive blessings—that is, during empowerments, feast offerings, and in the two phases of approach and accomplishment (in a sadhana)—he must mainly uphold the mantra vows in which the two lower vows are enhanced (as to their purpose and remedial quality). For example, with regard to the third empowerment, if the Vajrayāna monk is not free from desire and lust, he has diverged from the path of mantra. But if his seminal fluid is stabilized and is not lost, and if he does not apprehend the three doors in the ordinary way, there is no basis for the downfall of impure conduct, because ordinary desire—which is something that should be halted—has been overcome. If there is no difference between gold and stone, the downfall of touching gold cannot occur. The present situation is similar.

It could be objected that the downfall of impure conduct is nevertheless associated with a material act,[25] for it occurs through sexual congress. This, however, is a downfall only for those practitioners who are without wisdom and lack skill in methods. In truth, a material act and its motivating intention are not separable from each other. Since they are not divided, when sexual intercourse is associated with extraordinary methods and wisdom, no fault is incurred. In the same way, one may take poison to which a mantra has not been applied and perish therefrom, or one may partake of poison to which a mantra *has* been applied and consequently remain unharmed. As it is said in the *Guhyagarbha*,

> If one engages in the acts of "union" and "liberation,"
> Knowing them to be illusions, tricks of sight,
> One will not incur the slightest stain.

Consequently, that which is a real downfall for a śrāvaka monk is not so (for it is eclipsed) in the case of a person for whom the three vows are gradually and qualitatively enhanced. The purpose of the vow is achieved in a more effective way. Furthermore, the causes, which are said to produce the downfall in the case of a śrāvaka monk, are not complete in the case of the monk practitioner of the Mantrayāna owing to his use of the extraordinary skillful methods. For the latter does not consider himself and his consort to be an ordinary man and woman. He visualizes himself and his consort as deities and purifies the sexual organs by recognizing them as vajra and lotus.

It might be thought that this disagrees with the *Lamp for the Path to Enlightenment* where [Atiśa] says that "The secret and the wisdom empowerments should not be taken by those who practice pure conduct or celibacy." But the teaching of this text was given with a view to those of lesser capacity. In the *Sacred Primordial Buddha Tantra* it is said that such teachings are given in the beginning in order to attend to the needs of those of lesser mental power (such as the rishi Sūryaratha) who cast the profound meaning far away. It was taught so that people like this might [gradually] enter the mantra path. On the other hand, it is in the nature of things that a monk practitioner of the Mantrayāna who has not received all the four empowerments is unable to attain buddhahood. He must therefore receive them all and rely on both the path of liberation and the path of skillful means.[26] The point behind the teaching that those who observe pure conduct should refrain from taking the secret and wisdom empowerments is that those of lesser aptitude, who [mistakenly] think that the practice associated with these empowerments will lead them to purity and freedom, should not in fact take them. They are forbidden to take such empowerments in the beginning. This, however, does not mean that such empowerments are forbidden definitively and for everyone. When in former times, Atiśa visited Tibet, the members of the ordained saṅgha had become rather lax in their conduct.[27] And his purpose in giving such counsel was to remedy this situation. It should be understood, however, that such advice is overruled by the earlier statement [in the Kālacakra] that the monk is the supreme support for the practice of mantra.

This matter is further illustrated by the principle [the fifth in the list given] that the three vows do not essentially contradict one another. When one is practicing on the path of the third empowerment, if, through the experience of blissful melting, the bliss of body and mind is fully developed; if desire is cleansed; if the seminal fluid is stabilized and not lost; and if the practitioner experiences no lust on seeing a woman, even though he may be practicing the path of the third empowerment, then the vows of individual liberation are kept and observed in a superior manner. As it is said in the *Guhyagarbha*,

> In the supreme and unsurpassed samaya pledge,
> The Vinaya discipline
> And all the many vows without exception
> Find their pure embodiment.

Moreover, after Saraha took to wife the arrow maker's daughter, he said,

> Till yesterday I was a Brahmin,
> Till yesterday I was not a monk.
> But as from now, I am indeed a monk,
> A supreme monk and a glorious heruka.

And it was after this that Saraha became the ordaining abbot of Nāgārjuna himself.

Furthermore, in the Mantrayāna, all the pleasures of the senses— such as the consumption of alcohol, the eating of food after noon, singing and dancing—are all enjoyed on occasions when they are the best way to complete the two accumulations and to eliminate the two obscuring veils. It is for exactly the same purpose that sense pleasures are discarded in the implementation of the other vows. As it is said in the *Twenty Stanzas on the Bodhichitta Vow*,

> When you are in possession of great skillful means,
> Defilement is conducive to enlightenment.

All three vows arrest and prevent the growth of defects and

faults, but they do not halt the development of good qualities. Moreover, when all phenomenal appearance manifests as great bliss, all the bodhichitta vows (such as those of relative bodhichitta in intention and action) are perfectly fulfilled. It is said in the *Hevajra Tantra*,

> Give rise to bodhichitta endowed with form,
> Both relative and ultimate.
> The relative is like the kunda flower;
> The ultimate retains the form of bliss.

According to the third principle in the list, the vows are transmuted. It is said in the *Secret Crown Tantra*,

> For thus we may observe that copper
> Is derived from stone; from copper, gold.
> When copper has been smelted out, the stone is gone.
> Transmuted into gold, the copper is no more.
> The Buddha has not taught
> That prātimokṣa and the bodhichitta vow
> Remain within the minds
> Of "inner monks," the vidyādharas.

When the level of tantric vidyādhara is attained, the prātimokṣa vows and bodhichitta vows do not persist in the mind as different and separate entities, for they are transmuted into the substance of the Mantrayāna vow. Nevertheless, the specific aspects of the three vows remain distinct; they do not merge into one. For when taking the prātimokṣa vows, one promises for the duration of one's life to prevent the deterioration of the vows one has received. And it is not said that the reception of the mantra vows causes the prātimokṣa vows to be relinquished. As for the vows of bodhichitta, one pledges to keep them until the gaining of the essence of enlightenment. And the receiving of the mantra vows is not said to be the condition for the degeneration of the bodhichitta vows and the cause for their relinquishment.

Since they come to be of the same substance as the mantra vow, however, this means that the vows of prātimokṣa and bodhichitta are transmuted. Nevertheless, their specific aspects do not merge and are not mixed up together. They remain distinct and persist until a circumstance occurs through which they are destroyed from the point of view of the respective commitments taken. Accordingly, it is explained that there are two actual causes (death and the returning of the precepts) and seven other factors that lead to the relinquishment of the prātimokṣa vows. Similarly, there are four black factors (such as to deceive those who are worthy of respect)[28] that lead to the abandonment of the bodhichitta vows. This point is explained in *The Great Chariot*.[29]

The fourth principle is that the three vows are gradually and qualitatively enhanced. The vows of individual liberation and the bodhichitta vows are included within the mantra vows in the same way that two measures of something are included within three measures (of the same substance). The *Māyājāla Tantra* says,

> In the unsurpassed and supreme vow,
> The discipline of Vinaya and the bodhichitta precepts,
> All without exception,
> Find their pure embodiment.

And the *Lotus Crown Tantra* says,

> The yogi who pursues the pathway
> Of the third empowerment
> Is said to be a great monk.
> He is keeping all three vows.

Finally, the sixth principle is that the observance of the vows should chiefly be appropriate to the moment. When one is engaged in secret practice, one must keep oneself from the downfalls that are considered differently at the various levels of the three vows. One must neither mix them up nor disparage the observances of the lower vows. If the observances of the three vows are in conflict, the person concerned must chiefly act according to the Mantra point of view, thus enhancing [the lower vows] as to their purpose and remedial function. When, however, one is in a public situation, one should guard against all the downfalls viewed differently at the three levels of the vows, separately and without confusing them. And if the observances are in conflict, one should principally act according to the two lower vows. For the Mantra view is very secret, and to act with such discretion enhances the purpose of not causing others to lose faith.

These six principles constitute an outline of the three vows and should be regarded as a most precious treasure for practitioners of the Secret Mantra who are holders of the three vows.

Those who are well disciplined by the three vows are counseled in the following way.

> 4. Beginners in the practice must
> First accomplish their own benefit.
> They should guard their minds in solitude,
> Forsaking busy and distracting occupations.
> They should rid themselves of adverse circumstances,
> Taming their defilements through the use of antidotes.
> Without confusing view and action,
> They should give themselves to meditation.
> Whichever of the five defilements
> Comes to birth within their minds,
> They should seize it mindfully
> And use the antidote without distraction.
> They should be careful, vigilant
> And have a sense of shame and decency
> In acts of body, speech, and mind.
> Let them thereby discipline their minds.

Beginners on the path to liberation should practice chiefly to secure their own good. They should strive for the benefit of others only indirectly through their aspirations, for as yet they do not have the power to achieve it. This is because the defilements in their own minds will create adverse conditions [for altruistic action]. Instead, they should remain in solitude and apply the antidotes to their own defilements, and they should practice without muddling their view and action.[30] They should focus mindfully on whatever defilement presents itself in their minds, so that it does not continue into the next moment. It is extremely important that they advert to the actions of their three doors with mindfulness, vigilant introspection, and carefulness. As it is said in *The Way of the Bodhisattva*,

> All you who would protect your minds,
> Maintain your mindfulness and introspection;
> Guard them both, at cost of life and limb,
> I join my hands, beseeching you.[31]

Advice is now given on how beginners, whose minds are under the sway of external circumstances, should deal with the various situations and experiences that arise.

> 5. Praise and blame, refusal and acceptance,
> Pleasant and unpleasant—let them see all these as equal.
> All, like magic shows and dreams, lack true existence.
> They should think of them as all the same—
> As just an echo's sound—and practice patience,
> Examining the mind that clings to "I" and "self."
> In brief, in all their actions let them not do anything
> That contravenes the Dharma.
> They should restrain their minds and do no harm to others.
> Not indulging in defilement even for an instant,
> Let them spend their days and nights in virtue.
> This is of the highest moment.

When one experiences praise or abuse, happiness or fear, one should remember that all outer appearances and inner experience are but dreams and illusions, and that they are without real existence, like the sound of an echo. One should examine for oneself that, being without shape or color, the anger and torment of one's mind cannot be found. As it is said in *The Way of the Bodhisattva*, "With things that in this way are empty, what is there to gain and what to lose?" "What is there to give me joy and pain?" and "May beings like myself discern and grasp that all things have the character of space!"[32]

In short, in whatever one does, day or night, one should exclusively tame one's mind. It is thus that one will refrain from harming others. Defilements will subside all by themselves and virtue will naturally increase. This is the very definition of training in the Buddhadharma. It is as Nāgārjuna has said,

> Tame your mind. The Bhagavān has said
> That mind indeed is Dharma's root.

And it is said in the *Prātimokṣa-sūtra*,

> Abandon every evil deed
> And practice virtue well.
> Perfectly subdue your mind:
> This is Buddha's teaching.

The proof of the validity of what has been said begins with the advice that one should not lose sight of one's own personal objective, since it is difficult at the beginning to accomplish the welfare of others.

> 6. Since in these present, evil times
> People are uncouth and wild,
> It is of great importance to secure
> Your goal by practicing in solitude.

Unless the bird is fully fledged it cannot fly;
So too, unless you have clairvoyant knowledge,
No help can you provide for others.
Make efforts therefore to secure your goal,
And in your mind aspire to be of benefit to others.
Do not let your mind be lured by busy pastimes;
These are the deceitful tricks of Māra.
It is crucial to strive heartily in practice
So that in the hour of death
You will not be tormented by regret.

Even if the Buddha himself were to appear, he would be unable to tame the beings of the present age! Therefore, for people like me, even though we have the desire to be of help to others, the time for the implementation of this wish has not yet arrived. For we lack preternatural knowledge and the power of working miracles, and it is impossible to benefit beings by force. Under these circumstances, work for the good of others cannot be other than an idle show, and people should not be advised to engage in it. They should instead be encouraged to practice one-pointedly in forest solitudes. The seductions of Māra, the distractions and busyness of this life have already deceived us in the past. By now we have had enough of it. We should, in all sincerity, go away, alone, to solitary places and persevere in securing our own benefit so that at the time of death, we will not be tormented by remorse [at the missed opportunity]. Now is the time for cultivating in our minds the *wish* to be of benefit to others. It is as Śāntideva has said,

So many are the leanings and the wants of beings
That even Buddha could not please them all—
Of such a wretch as me, no need to speak![33]

Still, even though one begins by practicing in one's own interest, it is difficult to remain focused on this, and therefore one is advised to invest all one's efforts in the enterprise.

7. Now therefore inspect your mind!
Look! If now you were to die, how would you fare?
There's nothing sure in where you'll go
And what you will become.
By spending nights and days deceived in your distractions,
You meaninglessly waste your freedoms and advantages.
Meditate alone in solitude on the essential teachings.
Strive now to gain your ultimate objective.
Do you know where you will go at death?
Make effort therefore in this very instant.

Turn and look within yourself. If you were to die in this present moment, is your mind ready to depart for a happy destination or not? It is important to reflect that in frittering away your days and nights in distraction, your freedoms and advantages are wasted. For it is in this present moment that you must work to secure the ultimate objective of your enlightenment. It is in the here and now that you should sincerely strive in the practice of Dharma. As we find in *The Way of the Bodhisattva*,

And yet the way I act is such
That I shall not regain a human life!
And losing this, my precious human form,
My evils will be many, virtues none.[34]

Hard to bear are the hallucinatory experiences of saṃsāra! Therefore one is advised to strive to free oneself from them in this very moment.

8. Saṃsāra's false appearances
Are like a dangerous pathway filled with fear.
Remember! You must find a way to free yourself.
If once again you are beguiled,
You will forever wander in delusion.
Give rise to constancy therefore and keep it in your heart!

The thought of the sufferings of the higher and lower realms of saṃsāra makes one tremble with fear. They are like a difficult and terrifying path or a gigantic precipice. If one is unable to escape it, no freedom will ever be possible. Therefore one must persevere. As Śāntideva says,

> Along a small and ordinary cliff
> If I must pick my way with special care,
> What need to speak of that long-lasting chasm
> Plunging to the depths a thousand leagues?[35]

Again it is taught that it is essential to be diligent in the practice of the Dharma. For it is hard to cross the ocean of saṃsāra.

> 9. Now in your boat of freedoms and advantages
> Traverse that ocean hard to cross:
> Defilement and your clinging to a "self."
> Thanks to the power of your merit,
> Your one-in-a-hundred chance has dawned:
> Your path to liberation and enlightenment!
> So now, and with wholehearted constancy,
> Secure your happiness and benefit!

Defilement is like a deep ocean, and one's present freedoms and advantages are like a boat with which to cross it. Again, as *The Way of the Bodhisattva* says,

> This vessel will be later hard to find.
> The time that you have now, you fool, is not for sleep![36]

These freedoms and advantages, so hard to find, have now been found, and the respective defects and qualities of saṃsāra and nirvāṇa have been understood. Moreover, the little thought "I must practice the Dharma" has occurred. This is a sign that the Buddha's compassion has entered one's heart. It is like a flash of lightning in deep darkness. For it is not easy for such a virtuous state of mind to arise. Now that it has occurred, it should be pursued with diligence and without delay. As *The Way of the Bodhisattva* says,

> So hard to find the ease and wealth
> Whereby the aims of beings may be gained.
> If now I fail to turn it to my profit,
> How could such a chance be mine again?

> Just as on a dark night black with clouds,
> The sudden lightning glares and all is clearly shown,
> Likewise rarely, through the buddhas' power,
> Virtuous thoughts rise, brief and transient, in the world.

> Virtue, thus, is weak. . .[37]

Now comes the advice that one must be diligent in Dharma because adversity is always at hand.

> 10. Life is fleeting, every instant changing.
> Distractions, wise in tricking you,
> Postpone your virtuous deeds.
> So strong is your old habit of delusion!
> Defilements in their multitude
> Befall you naturally and in an instant,
> Whereas merit-bearing virtue hardly comes
> However much you try!
> So crucial is it then to strive
> To turn back karma's powerful wind!

The lives of beings are not permanent even for an instant. And Dharma practitioners are betrayed by the distracting appearances of this world. The childish always put off their virtuous practice till later. Beings in saṃsāra are so long inured to its hallucinatory appearances that, throughout the three worlds, defilements fall on them like rain. Positive action occurs but rarely and only thanks to the actions of the Victorious Ones. It is difficult to turn back the swell of the ocean of defilement. It is of the greatest importance to strive steadily in the Dharma with all one's might and to avoid sporadic practice. I request you to consider carefully the meaning of the words of the *Udānavarga*,

Alas! Conditioned things are fleeting;
They arise and perish.
Instead of simply being born and dying,
Strive swiftly to achieve the bliss of peace.

Finally there comes an instruction that, precisely because saṃsāra lacks any essential meaning, it is vital to strive diligently in the Dharma.

11. In saṃsāra, there is not the slightest joy.
Unbearable it is to think
Of all the sorrows in this wheel of life.
So now attend to methods that will set you free from it.
If instead of a sincere exertion
In the essence of the Doctrine,
You dawdle in a leisurely, infrequent practice,
No good will come of it.
So cultivate increasingly awareness of impermanence
Together with a wholesome sorrow with the world.
Gird yourself with effort in the practice.
Do not be distracted even for an instant.

It is intolerable to reflect upon the sufferings in the three worlds of saṃsāra. We must find a way to escape it. We should make unremitting efforts in the Dharma. It is not enough merely to understand and wish to do it. As it is said in the *Avataṃsaka-sūtra*,

Just as a skilled ferryman
Who has ferried multitudes
Across the stream then dies,
So too is Dharma if you do not practice it.

Just as a deaf instrumentalist
May be the joy of many
While himself hears nothing,
So too is Dharma if you do not practice it.

Just as the sight or sound of water
Does not quench the thirst
Of thirsty people,
So too is Dharma if you do not practice it.

Therefore, in conclusion,

12. If at the outset you have grasped this well,
You will in future swiftly come to the enlightened state.
And once your own good you have gained,
The good of others you will naturally achieve.
Now the supreme path you have discovered
Leading you to freedom from saṃsāra.
All that you do now accords with Dharma—
Thus you are the basis for attainment of enlightenment.

If you have a good understanding of the defects of saṃsāra and the benefits of liberation, and if you correctly grasp the injunction to engage immediately and strenuously in the Dharma, you will, through persevering in the practice, accomplish the benefit of both yourself and others. If you set out on the path to liberation with enlightenment as your final goal, whatever you do will be in accordance with the Dharma. It is said in all the sūtras and tantras that, in so doing, you will become the proper foundation for the practice

by which enlightenment is achieved. I therefore exhort you to act
accordingly.

In this circle of existence like a fiery mass of pain,
My mind in weary sorrow says to me,
"Now, in this life, be gone to peaceful forests.
Practice with sincerity abandoning distractions."

At this time, when my own purpose should be won,
To work for others would be just pretense,
A source of disappointment and of sorrow.
What purpose would it serve?
Therefore in the forest let me dwell alone.

In my present state, though I may strive,
How could I be of benefit to others?
When I reflect on inward life or outer circumstances,
Sadness grows, comes welling up.
So now in rocky heights I will remain alone
And leave there both my body and my life.

———————

This completes the second vajra point of *The Chariot of Surpassing
Purity*, a commentary on *Finding Rest in Meditation, a Teaching of
the Great Perfection*.

THE THIRD VAJRA POINT

An Exposition of Teachings to Be Practiced

This exposition begins with a brief introduction.

> 1. The teaching to be practiced has three parts:
> Preliminary, main part, and concluding section.

Each of these stages—the preparatory section, the main body of the teaching, and the concluding section—will now be explained in detail.

> 2. The preliminary teachings are set forth first.
> The outer preliminaries are the understanding of
> Impermanence and disenchantment with saṃsāra.
> These uproot from deep within the mind
> All clinging to this life.
> The particular preliminaries are
> Compassion and the attitude of bodhichitta whereby
> All practice is transformed into the path of Mahāyāna.
> Therefore, to begin with, train in these preliminaries.

In whichever way one meditates on the path of the Mahāyāna, it is important at the outset to reflect that one's life is impermanent and that saṃsāra is a state of suffering. Then in relation to this, one should cultivate compassion and the enlightened attitude of bodhichitta, which is to think that one will, oneself, attain buddhahood for the sake of beings. This is necessary because when one realizes that life is impermanent, one will not procrastinate in one's practice; and the recognition that saṃsāra is a state of suffering will break one's attachment to this life. Through the cultivation of impartial compassion, one will not fall into the attitude of the Hīnayāna; and by training in bodhichitta, one will come swiftly to enlightenment.

The special features of the Mahāyāna are the skillful means of great compassion joined with wisdom, thanks to which one will not dwell in either of the two extremes. As it is said in the *Abridged Prajñāpāramitā-sūtra*, "Without skillful means and wisdom, one falls into the path of the śrāvakas." And it is further said in the *Ratnāvalī*,

> Emptiness endowed with the essence of compassion:
> Such is the practice of those who want enlightenment.

And the *Abhisamayālaṃkāra* adds,

> Through wisdom there's no staying in existence,
> Neither, through compassion, in nirvāṇa's peace.
> Long is the path deprived of skillful means;
> With skillful means indeed it is not long.

And in the *Dohā* it is said,

> Those who embrace emptiness without compassion
> Fail to find the supreme path.
> Those who cultivate compassion only
> Stay in this existence and no freedom do they gain.
> Those who can combine these two
> Stay neither in existence nor nirvāṇa.

The superior preliminaries are as follows.

> **3. The following preliminaries are far superior.**
> **With all empowerments received,**

> You practice the two stages: generation [and perfection].
> You perceive your body as a deity,
> As deities the universe and beings.
> Thus you overturn attachment to the real existence
> Of what is commonly perceived.
> Thanks to training in the deep path of the guru yoga,
> Boundless blessings will arise
> Through the powerful compassion of your teacher.
> Obstacles are dissipated
> And the two accomplishments attained.
> So following the outer and particular preliminaries,
> Meditate upon the two superior ones.

Once empowerment has been properly received, one first embraces the practice of the generation and perfection stages. This is said to be the entry to the basic level of the path of accumulation[38]—the setting-forth on the path to liberation. Therefore, empowerment is the foundation of the path. When this is received, the actual path is described—in the common Mantrayāna—as meditation "on a single seat" of the combined stages of generation and perfection. However, in the present explanation, which accords with the Great Perfection, the visualization of a deity, together with the guru yoga and then the subtle yoga of the channels, winds, and essence drops,[39] are all classified as the conceptual, lesser, perfection stage and are taught as the preliminaries for the path of the Great Perfection. This general scheme may be briefly described first as empowerment that brings maturity and second as the generation and perfection stages that bring freedom. It is said in the *Dawn of Indestructible Light Tantra*,

> Many are the teachings given
> By the great Vajradhara.
> But briefly they are two:
> Those that bring to ripeness and those that bring to
>   freedom.

We will explain the empowerments according to their number, sequence, and Sanskrit etymology.

Regarding the number of empowerments, because there are four defilements to be purified, four mudrās of the practice, four experiences of joy, and four resultant kāyas, and so on, it is said that, for those who strive therein, there are four empowerments.

That there is a definite sequence [in the empowerments] is understood by applying them to the view and to the manner in which the support and supported are purified. First, the vase empowerment reveals that appearances and the mind are an illusion-like deity, and thus the Chittamātra view is realized. The secret empowerment reveals that phenomena do not dwell in any ontological extreme and are beyond conceptual construction, and thus the view of Madhyamaka is realized. The wisdom empowerment reveals the inseparability of bliss and emptiness, and thus the views of the first two inner classes of the Secret Mantra (Mahā and Anu) are realized. Finally, by means of the word empowerment, the awareness that transcends the ordinary mind is revealed as the enlightened mind,[40] and thus the view of the Great Perfection is realized.

When applied to the method of purification of the support and the supported, the sequence of empowerments is as follows. When one is alive, that is, when body and mind are conjoined, this same body and mind (the support and the supported) influence and purify each other. The essence of the body is the manifold of subtle channels. The channels are the basis for the winds and the essence drops, and the essence drops are the basis of awareness, namely, the enlightened mind. Accordingly, the vase empowerment purifies the body and brings it to ripeness. The secret empowerment purifies and ripens the channels. The wisdom empowerment purifies and ripens the essence drops. And the precious word empowerment purifies and brings to ripeness one's awareness, the enlightened mind.

The Sanskrit word for "empowerment" is *abhiṣeka*. Etymologically, the Sanskrit element *abhiṣiñca* refers to the cleansing of impurities, while *śikta* denotes the pouring-out of good fortune. In other words, empowerment cleanses impurities and instills good fortune. And one speaks of an *empowerment* because one is thereby given the power to come in this very lifetime to the vision of the truth on the ground of Perfect Joy.[41] The *Vajra Peak Tantra* says,

> The rite, the teaching, and practitioner,
> According to the ritual of the maṇḍala,
> Give rise to the mystery of perfect freedom
> And lead in this very life itself
> To the gaining of the ground of Perfect Joy.

Concerning the defects that accrue if the empowerment is not received, the *Guhyagarbha* says,

> If one does not please the teacher,
> And if all the empowerments are not received,
> One's learning and one's practice
> Will be fruitless and will come to nothing.

And it is said in the *Illusory Supreme Bliss Tantra*,

> If, without gazing on the maṇḍala,
> The yogi wishes, even so, to gain accomplishment,
> He is like a fool who threshes husks
> Or with his clenched fists strikes the sky.

On the other hand, the benefits that come from receiving the empowerments are described in the *Supreme Secret Tantra*:

> If one is granted genuine empowerment,
> One will gain accomplishment even without striving.

So much then for a general outline of the empowerments. The stages of the path that brings freedom consist of the generation stage and the perfection stage. It is said in the *Guhyasamāja Tantra*,

> All the teachings of the Buddha
> Are perfectly expounded in two stages.
> The generation stage comes first;
> The perfection stage comes after.

In the generation stage, by means of the visualized appearance of a deity on the relative level, the practitioner trains to eliminate all ordinary thought and to purify the aggregates, the elements, and the seven consciousnesses. In the perfection stage, through practice in accordance with the subtle—that is, the inconceivable—ultimate expanse, the conceptual activity of the ordinary mind completely subsides. The union of these two stages is defined as the path leading to accomplishment. It is said in the *Vajra Tent Tantra*,

> Through implementing the great mudrā,
> One attains the vajra body.
> By means of precious recitation,
> One's speech becomes the stainless vajra speech.
> In vajra concentration one's mind
> Will be realized as the precious mind.

And,

> Thus one talks about the *wheel of maṇḍala*.
> The method is the vow of bliss.
> The yogis who possess the confidence of being buddha
> Will not take long to reach enlightenment.

Without the practice of the generation stage, it is improper to proceed to the perfection stage. As it is said in the *Pledges of the Ḍākinī Tantra*,

> A path in which there is no deity
> Is a mistaken path,
> And as a mantra path it is unsuitable.

Although one's body, speech, and mind are, from the very beginning, the enlightened body, speech, and mind, they do not clearly appear as such, being veiled by one's habitual tendencies. In order to make them manifest clearly, it is necessary to meditate on the maṇḍalas of the two stages. As it is said in the *Hevajra Tantra*,

> The generation yoga is
> The aspect of the deity's form
> Endowed with color, face, and arms.
> Yet it removes the tendency to ordinariness.[42]

The benefits that accrue from engaging in this practice are described in the *Vajra Tent Tantra*,

> Those who meditate on such a buddha,
> Even if enlightenment they fail to gain,
> Will in their later births
> Attain the level of a universal king
> Or lordship on this earth,
> Or else to pure lands they will surely go.

Now that the general meaning of the two stages has been outlined, we must consider how one is to meditate at the beginning of the practice session. One may meditate on any maṇḍala that is appropriate, whether of a peaceful or a wrathful deity, belonging to one's buddha family. Alternatively, one may meditate on Vajrasattva (who embodies all the deities of the different buddha families) in union with his consort and recite his hundred-syllable mantra. As it is said, "To meditate upon a single conqueror is to meditate on all the buddhas." Why is this so? It is because all the buddhas are included in the five buddha families [peaceful or wrathful], which, because they share the same nature, come down to a single deity, and this itself is either peaceful or wrathful. The *Samputa Tantra* says,

> One should meditate on all the deities
> As a peaceful or a wrathful deity.
> A buddha is a dancer inconceivable;
> What power do I have to speak thereof?
> All are emanations of the mind
> And thus are of a single clan of adamantine emptiness,
> Which then becomes fivefold.

Then one should bless one's mālā. One visualizes it as one's meditational yidam deity and dissolves the wisdom deity into it. One makes offerings and praises [to the mālā visualized as a deity], and, reciting the dhāraṇī of dependent arising, one scatters flowers over it. The father-mother deities dissolve into light and melt into the main bead, which then transforms into the syllables OM AH HUNG. All the other beads are then visualized as the vowels and consonants, and, as one recites the mantra, one considers that from these letters there emanate the deities and sounds of the mantra. One should keep one's mālā about one's person in such a way that other people do not see it.

As for the mantras of the deities, some invoke the deities by name, others invoke them from their seed syllables, while others express the qualities with which the deities are associated. As it is said in the *Vajra Tent Tantra*,

> Just as when, with urgent voice,
> You call upon great beings
> Who, hearing you, will come,
> Likewise when you wish their presence,
> Buddhas, bodhisattvas, ḍākinīs, and queens
> Come instantly when they hear their mantra.

The mantra must be extremely clear. This is what is meant by the expression "attracting or gathering through mantra," which is mentioned in the scriptures of all the classes of Tantra. A single mantra purely and clearly recited is better than a thousand muttered indistinctly. One mantra recited without distraction is better than a hundred thousand recited distractedly without concentration. The *Supreme Secret Tantra* says,

> Pure recitation is a thousand times
> Superior to impure recitation.
> To recite with concentrated mind
> Is a hundred thousand times superior
> To recitation without concentration.

And in *The Way of the Bodhisattva* we find,

> Recitations and austerities,
> Long though they may prove to be,
> If practiced with distracted mind,
> Are futile, so the Knower of Reality has said.[43]

Once one has visualized oneself in the form of a yidam deity and recited the mantra for a short while, one imagines one's root teacher seated above the crown of one's head and surrounded by buddhas, bodhisattvas, ḍākas, and ḍākinīs. One makes offerings to him, recites praises, and makes confession, praying to accomplish one's desired goal. For the teacher is the root of all paths and the source of all accomplishment. The *Full Arising of Primal Wisdom Tantra* says,

> Through devotion to the teacher over months and years,
> You will pass through all the stages of the grounds and
>   paths.
> If to you the master is at all times present,
> From all the buddhas you are never parted.

It is also said in the *Arrangement of Samayas,*

Through unwavering devotion
The ground of Vajradhara is attained in six months.

And in the *Sublime Primal Wisdom Tantra* it is said,

Visualize your glorious teacher
As your crown chakra's ornament.

Guru yoga is necessary to prevent hindrances from happening and to ensure that realization comes spontaneously and one easily traverses the grounds and paths.

The benefits that come from training in the preliminary practices are as follows.

4. Through these four preliminaries,
Your mind embarks upon the unmistaken path.
And once you take this supreme path to freedom,
The fundamental nature swiftly manifests.
You will gain an easy skill in the main practice,
And there will be no obstacles.
Endless qualities you will possess:
Nearness to accomplishment and all the rest.
To train in the preliminaries is therefore most important.

Before settling in the natural, unaltered state of awareness, the enlightened mind of the Great Perfection, one must implement four preliminaries: (1) reflection on impermanence; (2) training in compassion and bodhichitta; (3) the visualization of phenomenal existence as a buddha field and deities, together with the recitation of mantra and the concentrations of the subtle yoga; and (4) the meditative practice of guru yoga accompanied by prayers addressed to one's teacher. Equipped with these preliminaries, one embarks without error on the path to liberation. The meaning of the fundamental nature will be understood, and it will be easy to implement the main practice. No obstacles will arise, and the supreme and common accomplishments will be swiftly attained. These and other excellent qualities will be achieved. Nowadays, many people meditate on this path without implementing these preliminaries. This, however, is a mistake.

Now the actual path will be discussed beginning with a short exposition.

> 5. Concerning the main practice,
> Through the skillful means of concentration
> On bliss, on luminosity, and on no-thought,
> The fundamental nature of the mind
> Will now be introduced to you.
> Luminous primordial wisdom, free from all elaboration,
> Uncontrived and coemergent, will arise.

Although kindling wood is not fire, nevertheless, it is through such means that fire is seen to blaze forth. Following the terms of the comparison, bliss, luminosity, and no-thought do not constitute one's actual awareness, which is self-arisen primal wisdom, uncontrived and coemergent. Nevertheless, if one strives in such skillful means—with bliss corresponding to the essence drops, luminosity corresponding to the winds, and no-thought corresponding to the channels—those who have received the pith instructions from a teacher for whom they have genuine devotion will, thanks to all these factors, recognize primordial wisdom. This primordial wisdom is described in the *Vast Display Sūtra*:

> Deep and peaceful, thought-free, luminous, unmade,
> The nectar-truth, this I have now discovered.
> Were I to teach it, none would understand,
> And so I will remain, not speaking, in the forest.

A detailed explanation of the path is now given under three topical headings, the first of which concerns the skillful means of coemergent empty bliss.

6. First the introduction through the skillful method of
   great bliss.
Following the preliminary meditations previously
   explained,
Imagine that three channels, straight like pillars,
Pass through the center of the four chakras.
The channel on the right is white;
The channel on the left is red;
The central channel is blue and like a hollow tube,
The top of which lies in the Brahma aperture,
The lower end lies in the secret center.
In the central channel, at the level of the navel,
There is the letter A, whence fire blazes, causing the descent
Of nectar from the letter HANG located in the crown.
This fills up the four chakras and the space within the body.
When bliss pervades the body,
The nectar from the letter HANG
Flows down without a break
Upon the letter BAM located in the heart.
Meditate on this until the experience of bliss arises.
Then the letter BAM gets smaller and more fine.
Your mind now settles, free from thoughts and images,
In a state devoid of all conceptual construction.
Through this method, blissful concentration will arise,
And thus the state of calm abiding.

The master Śrī Siṃha bestowed on the master Padmasambhava the
following instructions taken from the oral transmission lineage on
inconceivable bliss, luminosity, and no-thought. With regard to
the skillful means of great bliss, once one has meditated on phenomenal existence as being a deity and practiced the guru yoga,
one should visualize the chakra of great bliss, with its thirty-two
radial channels at the crown of one's head. The chakra of enjoy-
ment, with its sixteen channels, should be visualized at the level of
one's throat; the chakra of ultimate reality, with its eight channels

should be visualized at the level of one's heart; and the chakra of manifestation, with its sixty-four channels should be visualized at the level of one's navel.

The three pillar-like channels should be visualized as passing through the middle of these chakras. The white *roma* channel is on the right. The red *kyangma* channel is on the left. In the middle is the "ever-trembling" central channel, which is blue. The latter's upper extremity reaches the crown of the head and the lower extremity is in the secret center. The central channel increases in size. At first it is like a straw of wheat, then it is like the *ubhi* plant.[44] Then it becomes like a vessel for churning milk, and finally, one's entire body becomes the central channel, fine and transparent. Because the mind is focused within the central channel, whatever other channels one may be concentrating on, only the qualities of the central channel will arise. This is a crucial instruction.

Inside the central channel, at the level of the navel, there is a fiery *a-she*.[45] This has the size of a tip of hair, and from it there blazes a flame like [the hairs of] a horse's tail. When this touches the HANG (which is the size of a pea) in the crown of the head, a stream of white and red nectar flows from it and fills the four chakras and then the entire body. Specifically, one should imagine that it falls on the light-blue letter BAM in the heart and causes bliss to arise. When, through meditating in this way without distraction, one experiences a physical sensation of bliss, the letter BAM becomes smaller and finer until it disappears. And in the ensuing state of mind, where there is no thought whatsoever, one should rest in a state of meditative evenness. At that moment, and thanks to this key instruction, the indwelling primordial wisdom that is blissful, empty, and free from conceptual construction will manifest.

The luminosity of empty bliss that has arisen is now described.

> 7. A state of mind then manifests
> Beyond all thought, beyond expression,
> A space-like state beyond the ordinary mind.

> This is blissful, empty luminosity,
> The state of Great Perfection—
> Inconceivable and limpid dharmatā.

If one meditates in a state free from mental images upon the skillful means of bliss, the mind will become correspondingly blissful and a state of awareness devoid of mental activity will manifest. It will be limpid, deep, as open as space itself, and all-penetrating. It is thus that the blissful, luminous state of the Great Perfection, self-arisen primordial wisdom, shows itself. As it is said in the *Secret Sphere Tantra*,

> The mind cannot embrace the vajra of great bliss,
> Which is by nature the expanse of luminosity.

The experiences that result from this meditation are as follows.

> 8. As you grow used to this,
> Four experiences will come to you:
> All that you perceive is easeful.
> Day and night, you do not leave the state of bliss.
> Your mind is not disturbed by torments of desire and hate,
> And wisdom manifests
> Whereby the meaning of the Dharma's words is
>   understood.

Of these, there are three experiences that occur owing to the increase (both in quality and quantity) of the refined essential constituents.[46] These are the perception of everything as easeful, the experience of bliss by day and by night, and the fact that the mind is not disturbed by the torment of defilements. Thanks to this, one will be possessed of an extraordinary wisdom deriving from the experience of a direct vision of awareness and of stable, constant compassion.

What are the qualities that result from this meditation?

9. Through continued meditation,
The sun of qualities unbounded
Will arise within your mind:
Powers of vision, clairvoyant knowledge, and the rest.
This introduction to the nature of the mind
Through skillful means of great bliss
Is a crucial and profound instruction.

Through further meditation on inconceivable and empty bliss, one gains increased stability in it, and various qualities will manifest, such as powers of vision, preternatural knowledge, and the ability to work miracles.[47]

There now follows a teaching related to luminous and empty primordial wisdom that is free of discursive thought. First, it is explained how one should meditate on the skillful means of luminosity.

10. Second comes the introduction
Through the skillful means of luminosity.
First train in the preliminaries as before.
Then imagine the three channels
In such a way that *ro* and *kyang* have lower ends
That curve and penetrate the central channel
And upper ends that reach the nostril apertures.
As you thrice exhale stale air,
All illness, evil forces,
Sins, and obscurations are expelled.
And as you slowly inhale thrice,
The still world and its moving contents, melting into light,
Are drawn into the nostrils.
Passing thence through *ro* and *kyang*,
They penetrate the central channel
And then dissolve into a thumb-sized orb of light
Within the very center of your heart.
Concentrate on this as long as you are able.

Join the upper and the lower winds together.
As you exhale, retain a little air.
To inhale and to exhale gently is of great importance.
All the excellence moreover
Of the buddhas and exalted beings
Melts into your heart.
Do not wander from this state.
Through this method, there will manifest
A state of mind that's limpid, bright, and still.

As in the previous meditation on the channels, the lower extremities of the *roma* and *kyangma* channels enter the central channel, while the upper ends extend into the nostrils. As one exhales the stale air through them, all disease and negative influences are expelled. And as one slowly inhales, [one imagines that] all the three worlds of existence and all the excellent qualities of the buddhas and so on enter one's nostrils in the form of five-colored light. These, together with the winds, pass down and enter the central channel through the lower ends of *roma* and *kyangma*, whereupon they ascend and dissolve into the heart center. Through concentration on the central channel filled with the winds of the five wisdoms, a clear and empty luminosity, devoid of thought, will manifest. This is a supremely profound instruction whereby one gathers the whole world under one's power and swiftly receives the blessings of the buddhas. Thanks to this, wisdom and concentration will arise as never before.

The visualization required for training in luminosity is as follows.

11. Imagine that the radiance increases
From the light within your heart,
Which, setting the four chakras and your body all ablaze
And spilling outward, fills the world with light.
If thus you meditate both day and night,
Within a few days' time, your dreams will stop

And you will see these luminous appearances:
A moon, a blazing torch, fireflies, stars, and all the rest.
Outside and within, all will be pervaded by five-colored
   lights.
Because your mind is focused on the state of luminosity,
Calm abiding, śamatha, will manifest.

After meditating on the wisdom lights within the central channel, one imagines that the four chakras are filled with light, which then permeates one's entire body and spills outward. Holding the vase breath, one fixes one's attention on the five wisdom lights, which pervade all the worlds of the entire universe just like space itself. As the breath is expelled, one retains a little of the breath within and then slowly inhales. And as one meditates in this way, signs will appear indicating that the winds of the five wisdoms are held inside the central channel. A five-colored radiance will be visible around the meditation shelter. Countless displays of light will appear: blazing torches, the rising moon, fireflies, smoke, clouds, stars, circles of light, the apparition of deities, and so forth. At that time, both calm abiding (the mind in a state of complete stillness) and deep insight (the mind's naked luminosity) will arise united in a single nature.

One then concentrates on the utterly pure light.

12. The light then gathers back into your heart
And slowly lessens in intensity until
Your mind rests in the state of emptiness.
Not focusing on anything,
Your mind rests in an empty, clear, and limpid state.
A luminosity by nature free from all elaboration manifests.

The entire display of light is withdrawn from the four chakras back into one's heart and grows increasingly more subtle and fine. Then one rests in a state that, like space itself, does not exist as anything at all. It is thus that limpid and clear awareness, unadulterated, unfabricated, and unconfined, will manifest. This is primordial wisdom, self-arisen, luminous, and empty.

The luminosity that has arisen is now defined.

> 13. Such is primal wisdom,
> Luminous and empty, uncontrived.
> It is the fundamental mode of being
> Of the Natural Great Perfection.

This limpid state—clear, unadulterated, and unfabricated—is the fundamental mode of being of the Great Perfection. As it is said in the *All-Creating King*,

> Free of mental movement,
> Devoid of characteristics,
> Such is the state
> Of self-arisen luminosity.

The following experiences result from this meditation.

> 14. As you grow used to such a meditation,
> Four experiences will manifest.
> You will think that what appears
> Is elusive, transparent, unimpeding.
> Light will fill your days and nights.
> Your clear and limpid mind will be unmoved by thought.
> And free from the duality of grasper and the grasped,
> Knowledge will come surging from within.

Through meditation on the winds [luminosity], three experiences will occur. You will have the impression that phenomena are elusive and of an unimpeding openness. Night and day will be brilliantly clear. Thought will cease and a clear and limpid state of mind will arise. Finally, an experience gained through the

sustained recognition of awareness will occur: the duality of apprehending subject and apprehended object will disappear, and a vast
knowledge will manifest in a quick and nimble mind.
The qualities resulting from this meditation are as follows.

15. Through increased habituation,
Clairvoyant knowledge will arise.
You will develop powers of vision,
Perceiving extramental objects
Even when they are concealed by other things.
You will acquire the power of working miracles.
The introduction to the nature of the mind
By means of luminosity is the very essence
Of the most profound instructions.

Through training in the yoga of the winds, one will acquire concentration and, thanks to this, preternatural knowledge will manifest. One will acquire the powers of vision, such as the ability to
see things even when they are concealed—by a wall, for example.
In addition, one will acquire miraculous abilities. As it is said in
the *Abridged Prajñāpāramitā*, "Through samādhi, one will turn
away from the base pleasures of the senses and will acquire perfect
knowledge, preternatural cognition, and concentration."

There now follows a teaching related to thought-free primordial
wisdom, empty and aware, in which the stages of meditation on the
skillful means of no-thought are explained. Generally speaking,
the accomplishment of the thought-free state through focusing on
the increase in size of the interior of the central channel is similar to the previous two practices. More specifically, through the
three stages of propulsion, focusing, and refinement, one proceeds
according to the special points of awareness, and by this means one
is introduced swiftly and directly to the state of no-thought.
[A description is now given of the first technique, that of
propulsion.]

16. Third, through the skillful means of no-thought
The nature of the mind is introduced.
Meditate, as previously, on the preliminaries.
Then implement the three points of the actual practice:
Propulsion, focusing, and then refinement.
The practice of propulsion is as follows:
Imagine that within your heart
Your mind rests, luminous by nature,
As a letter A or else a ball of light
The size of your own thumb.
Then forcefully reciting HA
One and twenty times,
Imagine that the letter is projected
Straight up through your crown,
Higher and higher into the sky above,
Until it's lost from sight.
Relax your mind and body deeply
And remain in meditative evenness.
The stream of thought
Will, in that instant, cease, and you will rest
Within a state that cannot be expressed in thought or
    word—
An experience beyond the reach of thought
In which there's nothing to be seen.

One should then pursue the meditation as before [on the channels and so on] as far as the empty boundary of the central channel. Then a marvelous ball of five-colored light shoots out from
the crown of one's head and into space, higher and higher, until it
becomes invisible. One must then recite forcefully the syllable HA
twenty-one times and then relax one's body and mind.[48] It is then
that a luminosity beyond thought and word, beyond any description, will arise. One will also experience a space-like state, beyond
the reach of conceptual expression.

The second technique is now described: the focusing of one's awareness.

> 17. Now comes the stage of focusing awareness.
> With your back turned to the sun,
> Set your eyes upon the limpid sky.
> Stay still and let your breath relax
> Until its movement you no longer feel.
> And from within the state of no-thought,
> Freedom from elaboration will arise.
> A meditative experience of space-like emptiness
> Will come to birth.

When the sky is perfectly clear, one should sit with one's back to the sun and focus on the sky with an unmoving gaze. One should let one's breath flow gently. In the moment that the breath is held outside, an empty luminosity will arise. One will have the experience of a state of mind that is limpid and wide open—like the sky—without limit or partiality. For as it has been said, "As without, so within": the outer and the inner spheres are interdependent.

At that moment, the view of the "three spaces" will manifest. On the basis of the clear and empty outer space (the sky), the inner space, free of discursive thought, will manifest. When this happens, the all-penetrating and unimpeded secret space, naked and empty awareness, will be realized—perceived through a meditation that is endowed with skillful means and blessings. This is a supremely profound instruction of the Nepali master Kamalaśīla.

Finally the third technique is now described: the refining of everything into naked awareness.

> 18. Then undistracted, fix your gaze upon the sky,
> And in the state of mental clarity,
> Where thoughts do not develop or dissolve,
> Meditate, considering that the earth and stones,

The hills and rocky crags,
The universe and beings in their entirety
Become the same as space, an unimpeded openness.
You have no apprehension
Even of your body as a gross, real form.
Settle in the state where space and your own mind
Are indistinguishable.
There is no recognition of an outer or an inner world
Or of something in between.
And in that state of space,
Relax deep down your body and your mind.
Memories and thoughts—all mental movement—
Come naturally to rest.
With no thoughts spreading and dissolving,
The mind stays in its natural state—
The ultimate condition of phenomena
And the mind beyond all thought and word
Are, at that time, not two.
A realization similar to space now dawns.
This is the essential nature of the Conquerors
Past, present, and to come.

As one's awareness is focused on the sky, it will become spacious and empty, and at that time, one will feel that all outer appearances, the earth and stones, mountains, cliffs, and so on—in short, the entire universe and its inhabitants—become completely immaterial. They fade into a state of openness and merge with space itself. Even one's own body fades naturally away and becomes like space itself. Everything is like the clouds that dissolve into the sky. The mind, free from the movement of thoughts, settles in a state of profoundly spacious, all-pervading wakefulness, in which there is neither an outer nor an inner sphere, nor any dimension in between. And the realization of the freedom from extremes, similar to space, spontaneously manifests. This condition is known as *the realization of the exhaustion of phenomena in primordial purity*. As it is said in

the *All-Creating King*, "This yoga is like the sky-path of the birds."
And the *Abridged Prājñapāramitā* says, "To see what this might
be, examine pure space."
The experiences resulting from this meditation are as follows.

> 19. As you meditate like this,
> Four experiences occur.
> All phenomena seem insubstantial
> For you do not have a sense of gross materiality,
> And day and night you do not leave the state of no-thought.
> Since the five poisons naturally subside,
> Your mind stream will be soft and gentle.
> You will taste the spacious nature of all things.

Thanks to familiarization with these three factors of propulsion,
focus, and refinement, various experiences related to the central
channel and the nature of awareness will occur. Knowing that everything that appears is elusive, ungraspable, and insubstantial, one will
have no perception of things as gross and material. One will remain
day and night in a state free from the movement of thought. Defilement cannot arise, and no matter what the circumstances, one will
be without hope and fear. One's mind stream will be soft and gentle.
Understanding that all phenomena are unborn like space, one will
perform no deliberate action and make no effort in their regard.
    The qualities resulting from this familiarization with no-thought
are as follows.

> 20. Through training in this third technique of no-thought,
> You will gain the powers of vision and clairvoyance,
> Concentration, and various other qualities.
> Through the union of skillful means and wisdom,
> Calm abiding and deep insight,
> You will gain for self and others
> Immediate objectives and the final goal.

Through training in the third skillful method (of no-thought), one achieves meditative concentration. Powers of vision, preternatural knowledge, and a kind of concentration that was previously unknown, together with the path of the union of skillful means and wisdom, and the path of the union of calm abiding and deep insight, will be achieved. It is thus that the temporary and ultimate grounds and paths and all excellent qualities will be achieved

This concludes the section on the meditative stages of the actual, or main, practice.

We now come to the concluding third section, which is a supportive armor-like auxiliary to the implementation of the main practice. Here is a brief summary.

> 21. In the concluding explanations
> Four topics are discussed:
> Experiences in meditation,
> Enhancement, realization, and the fruit.

This short explanation is now followed by one in greater detail.

The first of the four topics is a description of the flawed experiences [that may occur in one's meditation].

> 22. Meditative experiences are of two kinds.
> Those that have no flaw have been discussed above.
> The faulty kind come from attachment and fixation
> On bliss, on luminosity, and no-thought.
> These consist in clinging to experiences
> Of bliss, of luminosity, and of no-thought;
> In considering such experiences
> As objectives in themselves;
> In fixating on them in a faulty manner;
> And in mixing them with poison.
> Erring bliss betokens common lust,
> The loss of semen, and induces
> Mostly discontent and dullness.

Erring luminosity implies the wild disturbance
Of the winds and common anger.
It leads mostly to the spreading forth
Of coarse and agitated thoughts.
Erring no-thought is a state of common ignorance,
Consisting mostly of a state of mental dullness,
Of sleepiness, of lethargy,
And a blank state in the mind.
When erring states
Or flawed experiences like these occur,
You must identify them
And with antidotes correct them.

Through training in the manner described above, meditative experiences will occur that are either good or bad. The good experiences have already been described. Bad experiences are limitless, but in short they are of three types—resulting from mistaken attachment to, and fixation on, bliss, luminosity, and no-thought.

When one meditates on bliss, one clings to it. Thinking that the nature of the mind is empty bliss, one fixates strongly on empty bliss itself. One thinks that, aside from such meditation on bliss, everything else is a false path. One takes it as an end in itself. And one fails to realize that bliss is mingled with the poison of lust. These are five defects associated with the antidote.⁴⁹ In addition to this, there are five defects that are to be discarded. The erring experience of bliss is harmful to the seminal fluid and leads to its emission. An excessive lust arises and results in a loss of potency. When the seminal fluid is emitted, feelings of dejection arise. Since the essence drops are disturbed and turbid, the mind sinks and becomes lethargic. Finally, one becomes strongly attached to the object of one's desire.

When one meditates on the winds (luminosity), one must again contend with the five defects associated with the antidote. One clings to the state of luminosity; one fixates on the nature of the mind as being luminous and empty; one abandons every other path; one takes the experience of luminosity as an end in itself; and one is oblivious to the fact that the experience of luminosity is tainted with the poison of anger. There are in addition five defects that are to be discarded. These are the fact that erring luminosity is, first, harmful to the winds, causing them to become extremely turbulent; second, it causes an ordinary kind of anger to burst forth; third, it causes one's thoughts to become coarsely discursive; fourth, it stirs up the winds and disturbs their circulation; and fifth, it leads to a situation in which one no longer wishes to stay in the same place.

When one meditates on no-thought, one clings to the thought-free state; one fixes on the nature of the mind as being a complete void; one turns away from all other paths; one considers this state of voidness as an end in itself; and one is unaware that the thought-free state is tainted by the poison of ignorance. These then are the five defects associated with the antidote. Then there are five defects that are to be discarded. An erring experience of no-thought is harmful to the thought-free state [of nonconceptual cognition]. This void state of mind becomes the indeterminate state of ordinary ignorance. It is dull because there is no lucidity, and it is foggy because there is no luminosity. Because it is not stripped, becoming naked luminosity, the mind is just vacant. And in this state of a complete mental blank, which is void and unaware, all movements of perception come to a halt.

All together, this comes to a total of thirty erring experiences. As to the ordinary way of correcting them, it is essential to identify each one and apply the best antidote according to each case. This is easy to understand. There is, however, an extraordinary way whereby these erring experiences are corrected by a single key point, which is the recognition of one's awareness. Having identified whatever hindrance has arisen, one should, with strong devotion and prayers to one's teacher, invoke his blessings. One should then search for the source of the hindrance, for the place where it abides, and for the person who is harmed thereby. And when nothing is found, one should rest in the lucid state of fresh, nakedly spacious awareness. At that moment, every erring experience will subside into the radiance of awareness, and it is then that one becomes what is known as a "practitioner who recognizes obstacles as accomplishments." For indeed, all that manifests, all that occurs, every fault and every quality are but the display of awareness, nothing else. When one is well, this is the display of awareness; when one is unhappy, this too is awareness; when one is ill, this is awareness; when one is joyful, this also is awareness. Apart from awareness, there is simply nothing. If one can grasp this crucial point, one will be happy indeed. It was in this way that I myself eliminated all obstacles, and I am indeed a happy man! Whatever hindrances and undesirable experiences come one's way, they should be completely transformed into a virtuous practice. This is what practitioners need to do. If, on the other hand, they use other methods, it is said that they will be disappointed. This is a most important point. So whatever happens and whatever thought arises, one should discern within it one's lucid awareness. If one does this, then even if one goes looking for obstacles, one will not find them. Here I have disclosed a most important crucial point of the Natural Great Perfection, and I have spoken about it according to the way that I myself practice it.

The second topic in this concluding teaching concerns the skillful means whereby the (aforementioned) concentrations progress and are improved. There are two things to bear in mind: the correction of any defective experiences and the intensification of these same concentrations.

First, there are ways to correct flawed experiences.

> 23. For the sake of progress,
> Use skillful means to counteract
> Defective meditative experiences
> And intensify your concentration.
> There are three ways to correct
> Such flawed experiences.
> The best practitioners correct them

Through the application of the view:
All phenomena are mental imputations;
They are illusion-like and cannot be pinned down.
All of them, like space, are equal and beyond fixation.
From their own side, they are empty.
Confidently meditators settle in a state
In which they do not cling to anything.
Faulty and obscured experiences appear then
As the fundamental nature of the mind.
All hindrances are thus a spur to virtue;
All adversities are helpers to enlightenment.
On the ground of bliss, the mind is always happy,
And realization dawns like trackless space.

The best practitioners understand that all things are without intrinsic being; that they are like magical illusions.[50] It is thus that hindrances transform into the free openness of the ground nature, and the realization of ultimate reality dawns. All the phenomena of both saṃsāra and nirvāṇa appear in the manner of magical illusions and are, from the very beginning, without intrinsic being. As it is said in the "Indra Chapter" of the *Prajñāpāramitā in Eight Thousand Lines*,

And Subhūti said, "Sons of the gods! If there be a phenomenon higher than nirvāṇa, I declare that even that is like a dream and like a magical illusion. And just as it is like a dream and a magical illusion, so too are the phenomena of nirvāṇa, for they are not different. You should not say that they are different."

To be sure, ordinary beings abide in the illusions of karma. Yogis abide in the illusions of meditative experiences. Buddhas, for their part, abide in the illusion of purity. All phenomena are illusion-like. The *Victorious Nonduality Tantra* has this to say,

Through the various displays of magical illusion,
There occur, for yogis, the self-arisen,
Pure results of their accomplishment
And various visionary experiences.
For beings in the three worlds,
Karma and defilement—sufferings—appear.
For the tathāgatas there arise
The secret inconceivable of all-cognizing wisdom
Together with the pure and powerful
Actions of enlightenment.

Practitioners should understand that the ground, path, and result
are all illusions. As it is said in the *Ocean of Primordial Wisdom
Tantra*,

> From the very first, the ground lacks all existence:
> It is an illusion of a luminous character.[51]
> All understanding,
> Views of permanence and of annihilation,
> All experience in meditation—
> Everything that might arise—is simply
> The illusion of one's realization.

Practitioners must understand that all phenomena are the display
of the illusory generation and perfection stages. The *Ocean of Primordial Wisdom Tantra* says,

> The deity's body is illusory,
> Appearing yet empty,
> Ineffable, beyond discursive mind.
> Its appearance and its emptiness cannot be parted.
> It is beyond all ontological extremes,
> And yet its features are complete and not confused together.
> Thus the wise should understand all things.

Having illustrated in this way that all phenomena—which clearly appear while being unreal—are illusions manifesting under certain conditions, it is shown that phenomena are without true existence. Now in order to bring about liberation from the illusion of karma (that is, the three worlds), the illusion of Dharma is set forth (meditation on the path and the nonexistence of the personal self), the end of which is the illusion of primordial wisdom (the accomplishment of the state of perfect awakening). Thus we are instructed to understand the matter. The *Questions of Bhadra the Magician Sūtra* says,

> Illusions that appear through karma
> Are all the beings who live in the six realms.
> Illusions manifesting through conditions
> Are like the things reflected in a looking glass.
> Illusions that through Dharma manifest
> Are all the monks surrounding me.
> And I the truly perfect Buddha
> Am the illusion bodied forth by primal wisdom.

When, having grasped what is to be adopted and what is to be discarded, one trains in the illusory nature of all things, one should understand that all phenomena are beyond the extremes of existence and nonexistence. It is said in the *Victorious Nonduality Tantra*,

> This illusion is beyond both being and nonbeing.
> Even in the middle place it does not dwell.
> Relative phenomena are unreal; they are but magical
>   illusions.
> They are self-arisen: an unceasing play.

The illusory nature of all things is extensively explained in *The Chariot of Excellence*, which is my commentary to *Finding Rest in*

Illusion [the third part of the present trilogy]—which I invite you
to study.

Practitioners of medium capacity correct their erring experiences as follows.

> 24. For practitioners of moderate strength,
> Erring experiences are remedied through meditation.
> They acquire a lucid clarity
> By closely focusing their minds
> And holding them with mindfulness.
> They settle undistracted
> In the state of bliss, of luminosity, and no-thought.
> Since distraction and the lack of focus
> Are mistakes, it is important in one's meditation
> Not to be distracted even for an instant.

All defects of meditation arise because the mind is unfocused
and wanders in distraction. Thence come hindrances both for the
support—that is, the channels, winds, and essence drops—and
for the supported, that is, the mind itself. Practitioners of moderate capacity should be aware that there are general and particular
methods for correcting this predicament. The general method consists in recognizing, and meditating on, limpid awareness in every
hindrance that occurs, discerning its clarity in the states of bliss,
luminosity, and no-thought. In this way, the defective aspect of
the meditation appears completely and totally as meditation itself.
This is similar to the explanation given in the *Two-Part Hevajra
Tantra*:

> Just as the fire that burns
> Is the fire that restores [to health],
> Just as, when there's water in one's ear,
> More water will expel it . . . .

There are three special ways of correcting faulty experiences. The correction of the erring experience of bliss is as follows.

> 25. When seed is being lost,
> Imagine in the vajra vase
> The letter HUNG, from which a blazing fire
> Burns all the semen that is in the body.
> Meditate that none remains.
> This will dispel the defect.
> Apply this crucial point even when your seed
> Is lost through illness or the action of an evil force.
> Once you have destroyed all clinging to the bliss,
> Meditate on bliss as empty.
> Closely watch the mental state of ordinary lust,
> And without tampering with it,
> Remain within a state that's free from hope and fear.
> In this way lust will naturally subside;
> The blissful, empty, primal wisdom will arise.
> The feeling of dejection is a fault
> Arising from the weakened essence drop.
> To counteract this, meditate upon
> The blissful samādhi of blazing and of dripping.
> Predominating dullness is a fault that comes
> When the refined essential drops
> Are not separated from those that have degenerated.
> In this case, sit in upright posture;
> Hold the vase breath; visualize a light that fills your heart
> And the entire world. Then meditate on empty luminosity.
> By this means, dullness is dispersed.

When one meditates on empty bliss, there are five faults associated with the antidote. These derive from the mistake of confusing empty bliss with pleasure. If one watches the nature of this pleasure, it will become vividly empty. By meditating in this way, one will dispel the defect. Of the five defects to be discarded, if ordinary lust arises, a focused meditation on its nature will cause it to subside and to manifest as great bliss. If semen is being emitted, one should imagine that a fire blazes forth from the dark-blue HUNG in the vajra vase and burns up all the semen [contained within the body]. Through concentration on the fact that none is left, the defect will be dispelled. A predominating sense of dullness and lethargy is dispelled by meditation on the winds [luminosity] as was previously described. When feelings of dejection occur, one should improve the quality of the essence drops. [This is done by thinking that] from the short A [a-she]⁵² a fire blazes up and, by touching the HANG in the crown of one's head, causes a stream of nectar to descend and fill one's body. Again, as the fire blazes out as far as the pores of one's skin, it causes the refined essential constituents to melt, and one meditates considering that the body's interior is filled with bliss. This is confirmed in the *Two-Part Hevajra Tantra* beginning at the line, "By the blazing *tummo* in the navel." And it is further said in the *Samputa*,

> From a point no larger than a tip of hair,
> Rays of light flash like a thousand lightning bolts.
> They issue from one's pores and terrify
> The gods and the asuras of the ten directions.

The erring experience of luminosity is corrected as follows.

> 26. If you cling to luminosity,
> This must be cleansed into a state that's free from all
> fixation.
> If your mind is drowsy and unclear,
> Meditate on it as bright and radiant.
> If your mind is turbulent and agitated,
> With eyes closed, meditate within your heart
> Upon a light, a letter, lotus, sword, or else two vajras crossed.
> These go down and down
> As though fixed to a long, long rope,

Until they reach the golden ground,
The base of all the universe.
It is certainly impossible that this should fail
To dissipate all turbulence and agitation.
When ordinary anger and wild thoughts disturb,
Remain unmoved and they will all subside
In primal wisdom mirrorlike,
Luminous and empty.

When the defects that derive from overestimating the antidote—
in this case, clinging to luminosity—occur, it is through recognizing the nature of these same defects and through watching it that they subside all on their own, without leaving any trace. Of the five defects to be discarded, ordinary anger is dispelled by watching its nature. Dull confusion is dissipated by making the mind lucid and clear and meditating on it. If the winds are disturbed and turbulent, this defect can be remedied by closing one's eyes and meditating on the deity's seed syllable within one's heart. If there is a great deal of movement in the mind and one is unable to focus, one should imagine that in one's heart there is a lotus or a crossed vajra and so on. This descends as though on a stem or rope, down to the immensely strong golden foundation of the universe itself. If one meditates on this for a long time, the defect will be dispelled. There is no doubt about this.

The erring experience of no-thought is corrected as follows.

27. When an erring experience of no-thought manifests,
Not clinging to it is the key point that will cleanse it.
When this ignorant state of mind is recognized
And directly watched, it instantly subsides.
The primal wisdom of the dharmadhātu manifests.
In the case of dullness, lethargy, or mental blank,
Visualize within your heart a light
That shoots out through the Brahma aperture
And stays, at a bow's length, suspended in the air.

As you concentrate on this,
Your mind is freed from all activity.
This is a crucial and profound instruction.

When one meditates in the state of no-thought, the five defects
that arise and consist in a strong clinging to the antidote are dispelled by watching their nature. Now, as regards the five defects
to be discarded, it is first through watching the nature of an ordinary ignorant state of mind that the limpid clarity of the state of
no-thought is elicited. And in that very instant, the ordinary state
of ignorance subsides in the primordial wisdom of the dharmadhātu. As before, dullness, lethargy, and blankness of the mind
are all dispelled by eliciting a state of limpid clarity. They can also
be dispelled by concentrating on a bright light, shaped like an egg,
that shoots up from one's heart and remains suspended in space
[above one's head] at a distance of about a bow's length. This is a
pith instruction called "revealing the clear state of awareness." It
has come down to us from the master Garab Dorje.

This teaching, for practitioners of medium capacity, concludes
as follows.

28. In general, it is crucial not to cling to anything.
If you are without hope or fear,
You are free from every obstacle.
Resting in the limpid state—
The luminous and empty nature of the mind—
Where no discursive thoughts proliferate,
Then surely you are free from dangerous paths
Of obstacles and flaws to be abandoned.

When the nature of obstacles and of good and bad circumstances
is recognized, there is simply nothing but [the display of] awareness. By simply settling oneself in the state of awareness, empty,
luminous, and free of all fixation, one dissipates every possible hindrance. As it is said in the *Dohā*,

Whatever you may cling to, give it up.
When you come to realization, everything is just
    [awareness].

Practitioners of basic capacity may dispel hindrances in the following ways.

    29. Practitioners of lowest power
    Rectify their flawed experience
    By the application of a threefold conduct:
    Through ways of gazing, through material factors,
    And through auspicious links.
    The general way of gazing belongs
    To the seven-point posture of Vairocana:
    The legs are crossed, the gaze unmoving,
    The breath is slow, the hands
    Held in the meditation posture.
    The neck is slightly bent,
    The tongue's tip placed against the palate.
    The eyes gaze down along the nose.
    The wind-mind is thus held in balance,
    And flawless meditative absorption,
    Free from dullness and from agitation, manifests.
    For every fault arises from disturbance
    Of the channels, winds, and essence drops,
    And these in turn arise through the disturbance
    Of the key points of the body.
    Therefore it is crucial to maintain them undisturbed
    In meditative equipoise.
    Since all good qualities arise
    When channels, winds, and essence drops
    Are undisturbed and functioning correctly,
    It is essential that you understand
    The body's vital points.

Every obstacle and the inability to progress in the practice derive from the fact that one is ignorant of the key points of bodily posture and of when and how to focus on the channels and winds. Conversely, every excellence arises from the correct implementation of the key points of one's physical posture. All pleasant and unpleasant feelings and all good and bad meditative experiences occur through the good and bad functioning of the channels, winds, and essence drops of the aggregate of the vajra body. There is a story in the Vinaya scriptures that some monkeys, having once observed a pratyekabuddha, went off to a forest where some other monkeys lived. They observed that some of them were lying down, some were angrily aggressive, and so on. The monkeys who had newly arrived adopted the key points of bodily posture [which they had learned from watching the pratyekabuddha]. Amazed, the other monkeys imitated them and within a short time acquired the four samādhis and the five kinds of preternatural knowledge.

Consequently, simply by sitting straight and adopting a cross-legged posture, with unwavering gaze, hands in the mudrā of meditation, the tip of one's tongue against the palate, the neck slightly bent, one's breath gentle and slow, and one's gaze lowered, one will find that meditative absorption comes of its own accord. For the channels, winds, and essence drops are brought naturally under control, and one's awareness remains in its natural condition. At that time,

30. In yogic exercises
And the other trainings of the body,
A crucial point is to maintain
A state of unforced ease
Devoid of any agitation.
Another crucial point is that
The gentle way of holding breath
Will profit from the forceful one,
And conversely the forceful one will profit from the gentle.

> To practice in accordance with your constitution
> Is a matter of supreme importance.

Physical training helps one to strike upon the key points of the channels and winds. When engaging in the *yogic exercise of immortality* endowed with its thirty-two stages, and in other similar exercises related to the channels and winds, one should proceed in a relaxed and easeful manner without any physical agitation. This is an important key point. The gentle way of holding the breath will be enhanced by the forceful holding of one's breath, and the forceful way of holding the breath will profit from the gentle way. And both the gentle and the forceful holding of one's breath will be helped by the neutral wind.[53] This too is an important key point.

There now follows a specific explanation of the key points of the body in connection with the three meditations on bliss, luminosity, and no-thought.

> 31. In particular, when practicing on bliss,
> The crucial point is that your arms be crossed
> At the level of the elbows, and your eyes cast down,
> While focusing your mind on bliss.
> For practicing on luminosity,
> Your hands should cover your knees;
> Your breathing should be gentle,
> And your eyes should stare directly into space.
> The state of no-thought, on the other hand, is gained
> From staying in the seven-point posture.

When one is meditating on bliss, in addition to sitting in the seven-point posture, it is also a key point to cross one's arms, because this elicits the experience of bliss and brings the essential constituents and the winds under control. For the meditation on luminosity, one's neck should be bent slightly backward, one's hands should cover one's knees, one's breath should be slow and gentle, and one's eyes should stare directly into space. These are the key points for dwelling in the actual state of luminosity. The state of no-thought will be accomplished simply through remaining in the seven-point posture.

Three material factors may be adopted as remedies to obstacles or erring experiences.

> 32. Material factors are
> A place for practice suited to the time of year,
> Companions, and your sustenance (both food and drink).
> Adopt whichever helps experience.

Material factors that are relevant to the meditation on bliss include the consumption of nutritious food and medicinal and honey pills, as well as the companionship of a qualified mudrā, or consort. The things related to the meditation on luminosity include the consumption of cooling foods, and high-altitude locations that command wide views. In relation to the meditation on no-thought, material considerations include warm and dark locations, heat-producing foods, and a manner of conduct that is relaxed and slow.

There are three ways to correct erring experiences through the creation of auspicious connections.

> 33. Regarding the creation of auspicious links
> When dealing with the loss of semen,
> A thread of three strands spun by a young maiden
> And empowered by mantra recitation
> Should be tied around your waist.
> This prevents emission of essential fluid.
> When thoughts proliferate,
> The state of no-thought is achieved
> From swallowing a pill composed
> Of sandal, cobra saffron, and "great fat."
> In times of mental torpor, if you take
> A pill composed of saffron, camphor, bodhichitta,
> Concentration will be gained—the tantras say.

If, in the experience of bliss, semen is emitted, one should visualize oneself in the form of a wrathful deity and, while reciting the fierce mantra, one should make seven knots in a three-stranded thread that has been woven by a young girl unstained by sexual intercourse. One should attach it around one's waist and tie the end around the base of the vajra. If one sleeps with such a device in place, the solution will be found.

When thoughts proliferate, the experience of luminosity is dimmed. If, on an empty stomach, one consumes a pill made of white and red sandal, nāga's (that is, cobra's) saffron, and "great fat,"[54] meditative absorption will be accomplished.

Mental dullness and torpor steal away the experience of no-thought. These states are dispelled through the taking of a pill composed of camphor, saffron, and the white and red bodhichitta. This is detailed in the *Māyājāla Tantra*,

> Sandal, cobra saffron, and great fat—
> With these the mind grows naturally calm.
> Samādhi is accomplished.
> Saffron, camphor, and the bodhichitta
> Are materials of enlightenment,
> Space-like, indestructible.
> A practitioner who consumes Akṣobhya
> Will overcome old age.

We then come to the methods for enhancing the primordial wisdom of bliss, luminosity, and no-thought. This comprises general and specific teachings. First the general method is described as follows.

> 34. To enhance the unflawed states
> Of bliss, of luminosity, of no-thought,
> It is good to place your mind
> On any object that is suitable.
> Begin therefore by concentrating on an object,

And subsequently meditation will become
Spontaneously free of any reference.
This crucial point is most profound.
It is supreme and to be earnestly adopted by the fortunate.
To reject this method, dismissing it
As being endowed with characteristics,
Is indeed to take the path of fools.
Avoid this evil way of those who lack experience.

The support for the concentration on great empty bliss is the blazing and dripping of the essence drops. The supports for the concentration on empty luminosity are the different colored winds.[55] The support for the concentration on the state of no-thought is the pure [that is, cloudless] sky. As one becomes less and less distracted, when one focuses on these supports, all thoughts subside. Subsequently, without adverting even to them, one will naturally and spontaneously abide in the different states of bliss, luminosity, and no-thought—all of which result from this profound instruction. As it is said in the *Sūtrālaṃkāra*,[56]

Concentrate your mind
On any object suitable.
Then meditate that there is nothing.
Later, give up even this.

Some people say that there is no point in engaging in conceptual practice endowed with characteristics. This is incorrect. One should understand that such people are without the slightest experience of the practice and are not to be trusted.

The specific explanation consists of three parts. The first part explains how to heighten one's concentration on bliss.

35. In particular, the best way to increase
The concentration upon bliss
Is, by drawing up the lower wind,

> To pull the essence drops up from your secret center
> And let them melt, dissolving in your crown.
> Then settle in a state devoid of reference.
> Subsequently join the lower and the upper winds
> And hold the vase breath.
> Focusing your mind upon your heart,
> Remain within the unborn nature.
> You rest thus in a state of bliss and luminosity
> That's free from mind's proliferation.

When a practitioner of the highest capacity is in union with a kar-mamudrā or consort, and when a common practitioner takes the support of an imagined wisdom consort, the essence drops descend into the secret center. At that moment, by one's forcefully drawing up the wind, these same essence drops are gathered upward as if on a silken thread, and they dissolve into the syllable HANG in the crown of the head. The yogi then rests in a state that is free of all reference, and as he subsequently holds the vase breath, he relaxes in a state that is free of all mental activity. He remains in an inconceivable state of blissful and empty primordial wisdom. Regarding the imagined consort, the *Samputa* says,

> If yogis dwelling
> In a rough, uncouth society
> Disclose this practice,
> It will be reviled.
> In fear of this, they will confine themselves
> To practice with a mental consort.

This may be explained in slightly more detail. Visualizing oneself in the form of the yidam deity in union with a consort, one should imagine in front of oneself a very beautiful girl, and one should look upon her with desire for a long time. Since she is visualized as Vajrayogini, her secret space is empowered, and as one imaginatively joins with her in union, one considers that, as the fire blazes forth from the letter A in one's navel, the letter HANG in the crown of one's head melts and the essence drops flow down from it. This [imagined] act of union should be performed many times. Drawing up the lower wind, one should induce a state of physical tension, opening and closing one's thighs numerous times. The essence drops then gradually descend to the throat, the heart, the navel, the base of the vajra, and to the tip of the vajra and thence to the lotus stamens of the consort where they appear intensely white. As this process occurs step by step, one recognizes joy, supreme joy, absence of joy, and coemergent joy. If one feels that one's essence drops are about to be lost, or if one wants to arrest their actual emission, one should keep the lower wind in its place and forcefully press down the upper wind. Uttering the syllable P'ET, the imagined consort, the mother deity, should then push back the essence drops, while oneself, still visualized in the form of the father deity, should draw them up uttering the syllable HUNG. Exclaiming the syllable P'ET, one should at a single stroke draw in the essence drops through the opening of one's vajra, and with the syllables P'ET and HUNG, one should pull them upward, drawing them into the crown of one's head. Finally, even the imagined consort melts into the nature of bliss and is also drawn upward and dissolves into the letter HANG. Thereupon, even the HANG disappears, and in this state one should remain. Subsequently, one should practice drawing up the essence drops, spreading them, and so on, in the following way.

A brief instruction is now given concerning the key points of the body and the visualization to be performed during the descent, drawing up, spreading, and so forth, of the essence.

36. From time to time perform
The "vigorous shaking of the lion."
Draw down, reverse, draw up, and spread
The essence drops
And confidently settle in the nature of the mind.
Implement the crucial aspects
Of this yogic exercise

As you have seen them shown
According to your lineage.

A detailed explanation now follows.

> 37. For drawing down the essence drops,
> Perform the mudrā of embracing
> And, sitting straight, exert
> A downward pressure on your lower parts.
> Visualize that bodhichitta
> Is made to flow down from the HANG.
> And when it falls into your secret center,
> Focus on the ensuing bliss.

For the yoga of the "lion's vigorous shaking," one should adopt a posture in which one's four limbs are touching the ground and one should shake oneself. With one's neck bent upward, one should pull up the lower wind and with one's lips in the position of a smile, one should say HA softly. This instruction is generally beneficial for the entire procedure: the drawing down, the reversal, and the spreading of the essence drops. In particular, when one causes the essence drops to descend, one should sit with crossed legs and visualize in front of oneself the imagined consort. Making the mudrā of embracing, one should sit straight with torso erect, thanks to which a slight pressure will be placed on one's lower parts. In proportion as the bodhichitta descends from the HANG into the secret center, the experience of bliss will increase and one focuses one's attention on it. Thanks to this practice, the essence drops will flow down to all the important places in the channels.

> 38. Then reverse the flow and draw it upward.
> Hold your fists at the level of your kidneys
> And "join the ocean and the rock."
> Draw up the lower wind
> And touch your tongue-tip to your palate.

Rolling up your eyes, push down and shake your head.
Imagine that the essence drops—
As though strung on a silken thread—
Melt one into the next,
Till the crown of the head is reached.

The essence drops that have descended into the secret center should now be reversed upward. Sitting upright, one should press the fists of one's two hands into one's sides at the level of the kidneys, and draw in one's belly back toward one's spine. One should pull the lower wind forcibly upward and place the tip of one's tongue against one's palate. Rolling up one's eyes, one should hold one's breath, and pushing down one's neck, one should shake one's head like a flag. One should imagine that the essence drops are as if threaded on a silken string and that each drop dissolves into the one next to it, beginning at the secret center and so on upward into the crown of one's head and melting finally into the letter HANG. This is how one should draw up the essence drops. The essence drops should then be spread throughout the entire body.

39. For the spreading of the essence drops,
Act as you would draw a bowstring
And strongly agitate your arms and legs.
Then with your tongue-tip placed against your teeth,
Pronouncing *si*, hiss out your breath.

One should first make a gesture with one's arms as though one were pulling the string of a bow. One should then perform the yoga of "the lion's vigorous shaking." Subsequently, one should sit cross-legged and, touching the tooth ridge with the tip of one's tongue, one should expel one's breath, making the hissing sound *si*. The essence drops will gradually spread, reaching even to the pores of one's skin. Considering that the essence drops spread throughout every part of the system of channels, one should rest for a moment in an empty state free of discursive thought.

> 40. Rest now with conviction in the nature of the mind.
> Lie down upon your back
> With gentle breath, your mind at ease.
> Do not think of anything; do not grasp at anything—
> Rest in the nature free from mental movement.
> By this means, great bliss, enlightenment
> Will be accomplished without hindrance.

When the essence drops spread, one should lie on one's back and relax deeply from within, settling oneself without any thought as though unconscious—calm and comfortable in the mind's natural state. This is known as "confident settling in blissful and empty primordial purity." There are no obstacles to the one and only sphere [of dharmakāya]. One captures the expanse of ultimate reality, finding, so it is said, "one's true home." Then, sitting upright, one should meditate steadily on this very state. If, in ignorance of this practice, one just continues to train in the three stages— that is, the descent of the essence drops, their reversal, and their spreading—one will become what is called a "zealous practitioner who halts exhausted halfway along the path." Such a person fails to acquire certainty regarding the mind's genuine, fundamental nature—not only in the present life but also in those to come. This key instruction is said to be the greatest method of the Natural Great Perfection.

The second part of the specific explanation concerns the way in which one's concentration on luminosity may be heightened.

> 41. The best way to enhance
> Your concentration upon luminosity
> Is by means of breathing.
> The gentle and the forceful ways
> By which the breath is held
> Enhance each other.
> In particular it is crucial to combine in alternation
> The slow and gentle holding of the breath

Both outside and within.
It has been taught that one should train in many other ways
Concerning numbers, colors, touch, and so forth.
But here, through this unique instruction,
All will be accomplished.
This training is indeed the sovereign method.

If, after training in the gentle way of holding one's breath, one holds it forcefully, excellent qualities will freshly manifest. Conversely, the forceful way of holding the breath will enhance the gentle way. The crucial point is to hold the breath inside and then to hold it outside. And again, after holding it outside, one should then hold it briefly inside. In addition, various other ways are taught by means of which the experience of luminosity is heightened: for example, focusing without distraction on the number of one's breaths, focusing on the colors of the winds associated with the five elements, focusing on their warm or cold contact, or focusing on the different [visualized] shapes of the winds.[57] Nevertheless, these are all no more than techniques of concentration and cannot in themselves put one directly in touch with ultimate reality.

In this context, a method is taught whereby, by means of a single key instruction, the winds are bound within the central channel, with the result that ultimate reality manifests without any support or reference.

42. Applying all the key points of the body
As was previously explained,
Especially that of an unmoving gaze,
Breathe evenly and very slowly
Through your mouth and both your nostrils.
Relax completely in the "ordinary,"
That is, the natural, state of openness and freedom.
The key point of the mind is not to focus
Upon anything, but to leave it naturally as it is.
Lie down on your back and stretch your arms and legs.

Then shouting HA, fix your mind upon the sky.
Rest calmly then, without distraction,
Free from thought's proliferation and dissolution.
The wind-mind rests then in the blissful state
Of natural openness and freedom.
This is the door through which arise
All perfect qualities countless and unhindered.

Sitting with the body in the seven-point posture, one should breathe evenly and very slowly through both the mouth and nose, relaxing one's mind for a moment in a state that is free of thoughts. One should then count one's breaths. Since, at that moment, the winds are bound within the central channel, the result is that when one does not think of anything, the wind-mind settles in primordial purity. Then, with one's arms and legs stretched out, one should lie on one's back. Focusing one's eyes on the sky, and exclaiming strongly the syllable HA three times, one should hold one's breath outside. As one leaves one's mind in its natural condition, primordial wisdom free of apprehending cognition—in other words, the state of the exhaustion of phenomena in ultimate reality—will instantly manifest. This is known as the "Great Perfection, which is spontaneously present as the maṇḍala of the vajradhātu, the indestructible expanse." The dharmakāya, the state of Samantabhadra, is reached.

A prolonged meditation of this kind will bring forth excellent qualities.

43. Your body then feels light.
No breath is felt.
All movement of the mind is stilled.
The mind is luminous and clear
And there occurs clairvoyant knowledge.
Swift-footedness is gained;
Your skin will gleam and shine;
And concentration will arise.

Signs there will be indicating
That the wind-mind has now gone
Into the central channel.
This is a supreme instruction.
It is extremely secret, most profound.

One's body will feel light, like cotton wool. No movement of the breath will be felt, and all proliferation of thought will subside. The mind will remain luminous and limpid, and subtle clairvoyance or preternatural knowledge will manifest. The power of swift-footedness, as quick as a horse, will be attained. One's skin will become glossy and brilliant, and a new kind of concentration will occur. In addition, one will behold smoke and the rest of the ten pure signs.

The third part of the specific explanation concerns the way in which one's concentration on no-thought may be heightened.

44. To enhance your concentration
On the state of no-thought similar to space,
Deeply let your mind and body rest
And focus on an object single-pointedly.
As you fix strongly on this object
Free from all distraction,
All other thoughts subside
Within this one experience of this object.
Then even the idea of this object vanishes completely.
The appearance of the thing remains,
And yet there is no grasping onto it—
It arises, yet is empty.

Again one should sit in the seven-point posture except that one should look fixedly at something—an image of a deity, for example. At that time, all thoughts will subside in the simple experience of the deity, and then the thought of the deity itself will naturally subside and nonconceptual primordial wisdom, appearing and yet empty, will manifest.

Other important points now follow regarding the heightening of concentration on no-thought.

> 45. This is a crucial point, and in addition,
> You must train as follows.
> Focusing from time to time on some external object,
> Expel your breath and hold it outside
> For as long as you can manage.
> The state of no-thought will arise.
> Sometimes hold your breath within
> And stay unwavering and undistracted,
> Focused on an object in your body—
> Whether in the upper or the lower part.
> Sometimes leave your mind
> Just as it is, without support,
> Remaining in a state in which,
> Though things appear, you do not cling to them.
> On the basis of this crucial explanation,
> The wisdom of the dharmakāya, free from thoughts,
> Will, from within, arise all by itself.

Sometimes, as the breath is held outside, and as one is staring at a stone, a mountain, a boulder, or some such thing, the state of no-thought will occur. Sometimes, as the breath is held within, and as one focuses on the four chakras, on the syllables in the channels, on light, or on the body of the deity, the state of no-thought will also be achieved. And sometimes, through the settling of the mind without any support, in a spacious and empty state in which nothing is apprehended, the seamless primordial wisdom of equality will manifest.

The teaching on how to enhance concentration on bliss, luminosity, and no-thought is now concluded.

> 46. The general way of heightening the concentrations
> On bliss, on luminosity, and on no-thought

Rests in the accumulations both of wisdom and of merit,
The cleansing of all obscurations,
The practice of the generation and perfection stages,
And the most highly praised profound path of the guru
  yoga.
This instruction is supreme and ultimate.
The fortunate who wish for liberation
Should earnestly embrace it.

It is by acting virtuously that one comes to an understanding of
nonvirtue. Consequently, the accumulation of virtue and the purification of defilement are profound ways to progress along the path.
As the *Buddha's Many Deeds Sūtra* says, "By accumulating virtue,
one accomplishes one's wishes."

The third topic of the concluding teachings concerns the realization gained from following the unerring path of fundamental
reality.

47. The realizations that arise through meditating thus
Are all of the same taste.
They are not manifold; they are not different.
It is like those who come from three directions
And meet together in a single place,
And like the different flowing streams
That join and are as one within a single sea.
Bliss, luminosity, and no-thought—
Whichever of these methods one may practice—
When mental movement comes to complete rest
And in the nature of the mind, the unborn space, dissolves,
The enlightened mind, devoid of concepts
(Whether of existence or of nonexistence),
The sun of fundamental nature, bright and clear,
Will rise up from within.
In this realization, changeless and unmoving,
There is nothing to be added, nothing to remove.

It is by its nature the sugatagarbha
Commensurate with space itself.

Just as people coming from different directions all arrive and gather in one place, even though one meditates separately on the three methods of bliss, luminosity, and no-thought, the realization they produce, their destined goal, is exactly the same: the naked state, which is aware, empty, and utterly bare. Its nature is an all-pervasive awareness that does not exist as anything. It is pure, seamless luminosity. It is self-cognizing awareness. It is free of gross obscurations and subtle veils and is self-illuminating. Although awareness is at all times present in everyone, only those who receive the blessings of their teacher may experience it. By its nature, it is an objectless self-illumination.[58] This profoundly indwelling luminosity does not depend on conditions. It is a *primordial* luminosity and does not arise adventitiously. This indeed is what is referred to as the primordial wisdom of luminosity. The *Prajñāpāramitā in Eight Thousand Lines* says, "As for the mind, the mind does not exist. The nature of the mind is luminosity."[59]

What is luminosity like?

48. At that moment, in the ocean of samādhi—
Calm abiding and deep insight,
One-pointed, clear, immaculate—
Phenomena are like reflections,
Free of all intrinsic being,
Mirrored without partiality or clinging.
Their nature has been realized as
Appearances and emptiness in union.
Appearances are empty;
They resemble magical illusions.
They cannot be pinned down.
The vast expanse of realization
Of this union indivisible,

The luminosity that rises from within,
Is brought forth through this pith instruction.

The things reflected on the [surface of the] limpid sea are just water, nothing else. The reflections and the water are neither one nor are they many. Reflections appear in the water, and yet they cannot be grasped. And in the same way, various appearances occur in the limpid reaches of the nature of the mind. Nevertheless, the appearance of sense objects does not soil the mind, and the mind does not grasp at them. The sense objects appear to the sense consciousnesses, yet untainted by [the mind's] grasping, they manifest in the manner of magical illusions. For when calm abiding, the one-pointed mind, assumes a single nature with deep insight, genuine and lucid, appearing objects are perceived but are empty, because the mind does not grasp at them. This state is referred to as "luminosity that appears while having no intrinsic being."

It is said in the *Determination of Valid Knowledge*,[60]

Everything is gathered in the mind.
Even when the mind is free of movement,
The mind that, with the help of eyes, sees form
Is the sense consciousness of seeing.

Through whose power does luminosity manifest?

49. It is through the teacher's blessing that you see
The self-arisen primal wisdom, inexpressible,
Beyond both word and thought.
And in the moment of its seeing,
Timeless are the three times,
No difference separates the future from the past.
This is the Wisdom That Has Gone Beyond; the Middle
    Way;
The Stilling (of all thought and sorrow); the Great Seal;

> The Great Perfection of the quintessential ultimate reality,
> That is, the fundamental natural state
> Where, from the very first,
> Phenomena are all exhausted.
> It is mind's luminosity,
> The self-arisen primal wisdom.
> Many names it has received, yet all have but one meaning:
> Ultimate reality, beyond the range
> Of speech, of thought, of explanation:
> The enlightened mind,
> The space-like nature where saṃsāra and nirvāṇa are not
>   two.

It is thanks to the blessings of one's teacher that the luminous nature of the mind is seen. As it is said in one of the *Dohā*,

> When the instructions of the teacher enter their hearts,
> They see it like a treasure in their hand.

When one beholds this space-like nature, which is unspeakable, unthinkable, and beyond explanation, one understands that between past and future there is no difference, that nothing can be taken from this nature and nothing can be added to it. And seeing this, one is freed from every fetter. As it is said in the *Abhisamayālaṃkāra*,

> There is nothing to be taken from it,
> Not the slightest thing to add.
> The perfect purity viewed perfectly,
> When perfectly beheld, is utter freedom.

Although the vision of this fundamental nature of the mind is called by many names—Prājñapāramitā (the Perfection of Wisdom), Madhyamaka (the Middle Way), Pacification or Stilling, Mahāmudrā (the Great Seal), Mahāsandhi (the Great Perfection), and so on—the meaning is always the same: awareness, the all-creating enlightened mind, which is similar to space. As it is said in the *All-Creating King*,

> To the single nature of myself, the all-creator,
> Many names are given in the statements of my entourage.
> Some call me the enlightened mind,
> Some the space-like nature,
> And some primordial wisdom self-arisen.
> Some name me dharmakāya;
> Some name me the saṃbhogakāya;
> Some name me the nirmāṇakāya.
> By some I am referred to as omniscience,
> By some as knowledge of all aspects,
> By some as three- or fourfold primal wisdom,
> By some indeed as fivefold wisdom.
> For some I am primordial wisdom and the ultimate
>   expanse.
> But all these appellations indicate
> Enlightened mind, the single, self-arisen.
> 'Tis thus that those who see me, self-arisen, speak.

Now comes the conclusion of the third topic: this realization is a state beyond the ordinary mind.

> 50. Unconfined, beyond all partiality,
> Not trammeled in the snare of tenets,
> Free from the discursive mind,
> Nondual, perfect, great equality,
> The wisdom of the Conquerors,
> The vast expanse beyond extremes—
> This is what practitioners should fully recognize.

The vision of the fundamental nature is not attained through reasoning deriving from the different vehicles and the various tenet systems. For it transcends the sphere of words and conventional truth. It is beyond the mental images that are employed in aspirational practice,[61] for it is mind-transcending, nondual, and space-like. It is beyond all thought and explanation. How then is it known? As it is said in the *All-Creating King*,

> If the fundamental nature
> You wish to realize truly,
> Examine an analogy:
> The fact that it is similar to space.
> When you realize, then, the unborn nature of reality,
> You rest within the unobstructed nature of the mind.
> The space-like ultimate reality
> Indeed is indicated by analogy.
> For it is similar to space.

When one is implementing this practice by focusing on the key points, it is important not to tamper with, or try to change, one's mind. And since in such a state, all hope and fear, all effort and striving simply fall away, one settles in the bare, utterly naked state of self-illuminating awareness. As the *All-Creating King* again says,

> *Kyé!* O Mahāsattva,
> If you wish to realize the nature of your mind,
> Since this is accomplished by not wanting it,
> Do not linger in equality devoid of thought.
> Dwell naturally in a sphere without adopting or rejecting;
> Dwell naturally in the state devoid of movement.
> For such is the mind's nature as it is.
> In suchness are all things established,
> So do not modify this state of suchness.
> Do not meditate on something other
> Than the ultimate condition of all things.
> [It is yourself so do not look elsewhere.][62]
> The buddhas would find nothing,

Even if they looked for it.
All is done already—there's no need to do it now!
All has been achieved—so now there's nothing to achieve!
Don't think you must not think of anything,
Just place your mind in the condition of equality.

Kyé! Listen to me, Mahāsattva!
All the buddhas of the past
Sought nothing but their minds.
They did not alter suchness;
They did not meditate conceptually.
Their own minds, free from thought,
Were perfectly accomplished.
The buddhas now and those who later come
Will all achieve accomplishment
Within the thought-free state, equality.

The fourth topic of the concluding teaching is an exposition of the result.

51. The varying results of all these concentrations,
Fully mastered, are as follows.
In the immediate term, through union
Of bliss, of luminosity, and no-thought,
Countless qualities—clairvoyant knowledge,
Powers of vision—all are gained.
And on the final level,
The enlightened wish-fulfilling qualities
Of the three kāyas are accomplished.
The twofold purpose for oneself and others
Is spontaneously achieved.

By meditating correctly and gradually on the path, and through mastering the concentrations on bliss, luminosity, and no-thought, one will, in the immediate term, gain powers of vision, preternatural knowledge, and so forth. And in the ultimate term, one will achieve the perfect awakening of buddhahood. Endowed with the three kāyas and primordial wisdoms, one will labor for the sake of beings for as long as saṃsāra endures. Accordingly, from within the expanse of the dharmakāya, which is similar to the sky, one will arise in the rūpakāya, the bodies of form, like the sun and moon, and one will work for the welfare of others. As the *Sūtrālaṃkāra* says,

> Know that the kāyas of the Buddha
> Are all included in the triple kāya—
> The triple kāya is said to be
> Fulfillment of one's own and others' goals.[63]

And the *Uttaratantra* also says,

> The Knower of the World in great compassion
> Gazes on all worldly beings
> And, while never stirring from the dharmakāya,
> He appears in a variety of emanated forms.
>
> He takes birth in Tuṣita,
> And from that realm comes down.
> He enters his mother's womb, and then is born.
> He grows in skill in all the arts,
>
> Delighting in the presence of queens.
> He then renounces all and practices austerities.
> He then goes to the seat of his enlightenment,
> He overcomes the māras, and attains perfect buddhahood.
>
> He turns the wheel of Dharma
> And passes to the state beyond all sorrow.
> These then are the deeds the Buddha demonstrates,
> In impure fields, as long as this saṃsāra lasts.

And the *Abhisamayālaṃkāra* says,

> As long as this saṃsāra lasts
> So long he labors for the various good of beings.
> The nirmāṇakāya of the Sage is without interruption.
> And so as long as this saṃsāra lasts
> So long are his activities unceasing.

In conclusion therefore,

> May I take this path that leads
> Into the very essence of enlightenment,
> Immaculate and free from stain—
> This path that is the source of perfect peace,
> Of benefit and joy,
> This path that in the past brought perfect virtue forth
> Becoming thus the jewel that ornaments the world.

> A place of pure water,
> A place of flowers and sweet buzzing of the bees,
> A place where peacocks dance,
> Where lotus flowers shine,
> A place made beautiful and glorious
> By the ascesis of the wise—
> In such a place, in solitude,
> May I make the peaceful sky my roof.

> From existence in saṃsāra,
> That fiery ditch suffused with pain,
> May I with cooling waters of my stable concentration
> Lead every being to a place
> Of peace, of happiness, of freedom,
> And bliss without a flaw.

This concludes an exposition of the stages of concentration on which one should meditate—the third vajra point of *The Chariot of Surpassing Purity*, a commentary on *Finding Rest in Meditation, a Teaching of the Great Perfection.*

CONCLUSION

Now that this treatise is complete, there follows a conclusion to the book in general, beginning with the dedication of merit.

    1. Through the merit of explaining
    This quintessential teaching
    Deep and vast,
    A way of practice that will lead to peace,
    May every being reach enlightenment
    Adorned with two sublime accumulations,
    Enjoying endless riches of enlightened deeds
    Whereby to satisfy all wishes.

By the merits that result from setting forth this marvelous system of teaching and practice, may all beings attain perfect awakening, the state adorned with unbounded riches of wisdom and of virtue.

    The place, composition, and authorship of the treatise are now described.

    2. As a distillation of the essence
    Of the crucial points of his own practice,
    Drimé Özer, child of the Victorious Ones,
    For sake of those to come,
    Has well set down this lucid explanation
    On the slopes of Gangri Thökar.

Endowed with the rays of light of unstained wisdom and great erudition, [Drimé Özer] the spiritual heir of the glorious Lotus King, Padma Gyalpo of Oḍḍiyāna, composed this text upon the slopes of Gangri Thökar, King of Mountains. He did so for the sake of future generations, condensing on the basis of his own experience the crucial points of the pith instructions of the Natural Great Perfection. The readers of this text are encouraged to work for the sake of others.

> 3. You who wish for liberation,
> Be diligent in following my words.
> For thus you will perfect the two objectives
> According to immediate need and for the final goal,
> And swiftly gain contentment
> In the island of great bliss.

Those of future generations who practice in order to accomplish their liberation should strive in meditation according to the instructions of this treatise. Practicing night and day, they will swiftly gain enlightenment, the perfection of the twofold goal for their own and others' sake—thereby attaining the happiness of the sublime riches of the great bliss of supreme awakening. As it is said in the *Ratnakūṭa*,

> This enlightenment is the dwelling place of those who
> strive.
> It is not the abode of those who do not strive.

This completes the explanation of the conclusion of the treatise.

> May the firmament that is the minds of beings
> Be filled with clouds of merit that accrue
> From composition of this well-turned explanation
> And send down rains of happiness and benefit:
> The excellence of the twofold goal.
> May every being be enriched
> With wealth of manifest enlightenment.

Totally abandoning mistaken paths
And entering this *Chariot of Surpassing Purity*—
The sublime teaching of the vajra essence, deep and vast—
May all beings come into the city of their freedom.

This teaching is the day-star of a thousand lights,
A superb maṇḍala of texts, of reasoning, and pith
    instructions,
Which puts to flight the darkness of the mind
And coaxes into flower the lotus of enlightenment.

Repeatedly in previous existences
I cleansed therein the eyes of this my mind,
And in this life I mastered once again
The essence of the sūtras, tantras, pith instructions,
And became an expert in the meaning so profound.

When in the limpid sky of stainless discipline,
Intelligence with rays of light a thousandfold arose,
The many-colored lotus of the vast expanse burst into
    flower,
And light of freedom all-encompassing
Appeared in all the ten directions.[64]

Pursuing the tradition of great beings from the past,
In the footsteps of these perfect lords of men I trod,
And with empowering blessings of the self-arisen Padma,
On the slopes of Gangri Thökar I composed this text.

This *Chariot of Surpassing Purity*
Belongs to the tradition of the atiyoga, vajra peak.
Adorned by various wondrous words and meanings,
It is a supreme carriage on the path to freedom.
May all the fortunate take joy therein.

The Chariot of Surpassing Purity, a commentary on *Finding Rest in Meditation, a Teaching of the Great Perfection*, composed by Longchen Rabjam, a yogi well trained in subjects profound and vast, is now complete.

Virtue! Virtue! Virtue!

Appendix

A Structural Outline of the Third Vajra Point

Preliminary teachings
    The outer and particular preliminaries [verse 2]
    The superior preliminaries [3]
    The benefits of the preliminaries [4]
Main teachings
    A brief exposition [5]
    A detailed exposition
        Concentration on bliss [6–9]
        Concentration on luminosity [10–15]
        Concentration on no-thought [16–20]
Concluding teachings: supporting instructions for the
implementation of the main practice
    The flawed experiences of bliss, luminosity, and no-thought
    [21–22]
    The intensification of bliss, luminosity, and no-thought
    The correction of flawed experiences
        By the best practitioners [23]
        By average practitioners
        The general method [24]
        The special methods
            The correction of flawed bliss [25]
            The correction of flawed luminosity [26]
            The correction of flawed no-thought [27]
        Conclusion [28]
        By basic practitioners
        Physical posture and way of gazing [29–31]

Notes

ABBREVIATIONS

GP   Longchen Rabjam, *An Ocean of Elegant Explanations, a General Presentation,* in *Ngal gso skor gsum.*

TPQ, Book 1   Jigme Lingpa and Longchen Yeshe Dorje, Kangyur Rinpoche, *Treasury of Precious Qualities,* translated by Padmakara Translation Group (Boston: Shambhala Publications, 2010).

TPQ, Book 2   Jigme Lingpa and Longchen Yeshe Dorje, Kangyur Rinpoche, *Treasury of Precious Qualities, Book 2,* translated by Padmakara Translation Group (Boston: Shambhala Publications, 2013).

WB   Shantideva, *The Way of the Bodhisattva: A Translation of the Bodhicharyāvatāra,* Translated by the Padmakara Translation Group. Rev. ed. (Boston: Shambhala Publications, 2006).

1. *bSam gtan ngal gso.*
2. *Sems nyid ngal gso.*
3. *Ngal gso skor gsum.*
4. Respectively, *shing rta, phreng ba,* and *don khrid.*
5. *sPyi don legs bshad rgya mtsho.*
6. *Shing rta chen po.*
7. *Shing rta rnam par dag pa.*
8. *sGyu ma ngal gso. The Chariot of Surpassing Purity,* in the commentary to stanza 23, refers explicitly to *The Chariot of Excellence* (*Shing rta bzang po*). See p. 108.
9. *'Jig rten pa'i bsam gtan rtog med rang gsal gyi ting nge 'dzin khams gsum pa'i sems kyi spyod yul can.* GP, p. 97.

10. *'Jig rten las 'das pa'i bsam gtan gyi ngal stegs shes rab dang ting nge 'dzin zung 'brel khyad par can gyi zhi lhag sgom pa.* Ibid.

11. *Dus bzhi rnal 'byor gyi sgrub pa zab mo.*

12. *Man ngag lta ba'i rdzong phreng.* We have been unable to locate this text, which is evidently quite different from Guru Padmasambhava's more famous doxographical text entitled *Garland of Views* (*Man ngag lta ba'i phreng ba*).

13. For a full review of this intricate topic, see TPQ, Book 1, pp. 284–316.

14. *rang bzhin rdzogs pa chen po.* In this expression, the term "natural" (*rang bzhin*) refers to the fact that the "face" or "likeness" (*bzhin*) of ultimate reality is shown exactly as it is without any modification or elaboration.

15. On the ultimate level, Prajñāpāramitā and the Great Perfection are the same. There is a considerable difference, however, in the way they establish the ground, as well as in their associated meditative practices. See TPQ, Book 2, p. 436n454.

16. This is what the Tibetan actually says. The fact that it appears to be in contradiction with the previous description suggests a scribal error.

17. See note 17.

18. This expression does not mean actual infinity. It denotes a lapse of time, defined by Vasubandhu in his *Abhidharmakośa* as 10^{58} kalpas. A kalpa is a period of time covering the formation, existence, and destruction of a universal system together with a period of voidness preceding the formation of a subsequent universe.

19. *dag mnyam dkyil 'khor gcig.* This refers to the two superior truths of the Secret Mantra. According to the superior relative truth, all phenomena are pure in being the display of the kāyas and wisdoms. According to the superior ultimate truth, the ultimate nature of phenomena is the "seven riches of the tathāgatas." See TPQ, Book 2, p. 341.

20. For a description of the five Mahāyāna paths, see TPQ, Book 1, pp. 391–92.

21. The Tibetan for these six principles are as follows: (1) *rang ldog ma 'dres*, (2) *dgag dgos yongs rdzogs*, (3) *ngo bo gnas 'gyur*, (4) *yon tan yar ldan*, (5) *gnad kyis mi 'gal*, and (6) *dus skabs kyi gtso bor 'gyur bya ba*.

22. Each of the three sets of vows retains its own particular character in that the authorities from whom one receives the vows, the attitudes with which one takes them, and the rituals employed are all distinct.

23. They all serve the same purpose, which is to free the mind. See TPQ, Book 1, p. 297.

24. The text reads *thams cad log la mkhar rtsigs*, probably a scribal error. Khenchen Pema Sherab corrected this to *thams cad long la mkhar rtsigs*.

25. *dngos po.*

26. There are two kinds of practice in the tantric tradition. First, there is meditation according to the path of liberation (*grol lam*) and, second, there is meditation according to the path of skillful means (*thabs lam*). In brief, the path of liberation emphasizes the three kinds of wisdom (deriving from hearing, reflection, and meditation on the teachings). It is by this means that certainty in the view of Secret Mantra is achieved and applied to the practice of the generation stage. The path of skillful means, on the other hand, emphasizes method and involves practices related to, among other things, the channels, wind energies, and essence drops, thanks to which the immanent primordial wisdom swiftly arises.

27. It is said that following the period of persecution of the Buddhist teachings by King Langdarma, a teacher known as the Red Master and another who went by the name of the Blue-Robed Paṇḍita came from India to Tibet and propagated practices involving public orgies and killing. Many Tibetans were led astray.

28. The remaining three of the four black factors are to cause people to regret what is not to be regretted, to speak to holy beings with surly and unpleasant words, and to act toward beings with cunning and deceit.

29. I.e., the autocommentary to *Finding Rest in the Nature of the Mind.*

30. See the words of Guru Padmasambhava as quoted in TPQ, Book 2, p. 208.

> Great King, in my teaching of Secret Mantra, the view is attuned to the dharmakaya, but the conduct is in harmony with the way of the Bodhisattva. Do not let your conduct get lost in the view. If it does, you will understand neither virtue nor sin, and you will be unable to repair your negativities later on. On the other hand, if your view follows and keeps company with your conduct, you will be fettered by things and their attributes, and liberation will elude you. My Secret Mantra teaching is mostly focused on the mind; the view is the most important thing. In the future, many will have the certainty of words but will not have the certainty of the view and to the lower realms they will go.

31. See WB, chap. 5, v. 23.

32. Ibid., chap. 9, vv. 151, 152, and 154.

33. Ibid., chap. 8, v. 22.

34. Ibid., chap. 4, v. 17.

35. Ibid., chap. 2, v. 57.

36. Ibid., chap. 7, v. 14.

37. Ibid., chap. 1, vv. 4–6.

38. See TPQ, Book 1, p. 391.

39. For an explanation of channels, winds, and essence drops, see TPQ, Book 2, pp. 155–64.

40. For an explanation of the etymological meaning of the enlightened mind, or bodhicitta, see TPQ, Book 2, p. 236.

41. Perfect Joy is the first of the bodhisattva levels, or bhūmis.

42. The text should read here: *lha yi rnam pa'i gzugs kyis ni/ /bzhin lag kha dog gnas pa ni/ /skyes pa tsam gyis rnam par gnas/ /'on kyang bag chags phal pas so/ /*

43. WB, chap. 5, v. 16.

44. The stem of this plant has a diameter the size of a small coin.

45. This is the vertical line of the Tibetan letter A, which is pointed at the lower extremity and widens toward the top. In the present context, it is visualized upside down, that is, with the pointed end uppermost.

46. *khams dangs ma.* This is a synonym of "essence drop" (*thig le*).

47. For a detailed presentation of these qualities of enlightenment, see TPQ, Book 1, pp. 387–89.

48. It is not clear in which order the recitation of the syllable HA and the visualization of the projection of the ball of light (or letter A) occur. In both the root text and commentary, we have translated exactly what Longchenpa says.

49. *gnyen po las gyur pa lnga.* According to Khenchen Pema Sherab, "antidote" (*gnyen po*) should be understood here as a good quality (bliss) that is spoiled by these five attitudes.

50. *sgyu ma.* This Tibetan term is always understood in the sense of a "magical illusion," that is, a false appearance created by magic on the basis of substances that bear no relation to the resulting hallucination (for example, on the basis of a stone and a twig, the magician conjures up the appearance of an elephant). It is distinguished from the kind of false appearance that arises through faulty perception on the basis of objects that in some way resemble the resulting effect. For instance, from a certain angle and in a certain light, a pile of stones might look like a man.

51. *rang bzhin sgyu ma.* As explained in *The Chariot of Excellence*, the autocommentary to *Finding Rest in Illusion*, this expression refers to the luminous nature of the mind, the sugatagarbha, which is the ground of purification.

52. See note 45.

53. According to Dilgo Khyentse Rinpoche, the neutral wind corresponds to the fire-accompanying wind, the all-pervading wind, and the life-supporting wind, all of which are gathered together and held in the vase breath. By contrast, the upward-moving wind is male in character, and the downward-voiding wind is female in character. See TPQ, Book 2, pp. 161 and 413n288.

54. I.e., human fat.

55. See TPQ, Book 2, p. 162.

56. We have been unable to locate this text in the present editions of the Sūtrālaṃkāra.

57. See TPQ, Book 2, p. 162.

58. This means that awareness is free from the duality of distinct subject and object. That which sees and that which is seen are the same primordial wisdom or awareness.

59. This citation is traditionally understood to refer to the three turnings of the wheel of the Dharma. In the first turning (the teachings, for instance, on the four noble truths, the twelvefold chain of dependent arising, etc.), phenomena (here, the mind) are asserted. In the second turning (the teachings on Prajñāpāramitā, that is, emptiness), the real existence of phenomena is denied (the mind does not exist). In the third turning (the teachings on the buddha nature), the luminous nature of the mind is asserted.

60. Pramāṇaviniścaya (Tshad ma rnam par nges pa). This is one of Dharmakīrti's seven great texts on valid knowledge (tshad ma sde bdun).

61. Two forms of meditation are open to the practitioner: aspirational meditation (mos sgom) and "truly perfect" meditation (lam nges rdzogs). In the first case, when one is unused to the practice of visualizing oneself as a deity, and one thinks, "I am the deity" or "the deity is like this or like that," this same deity appears to one's mind in a conceptual manner, like any other abstract idea. This is referred to as the manifestation of the deity in terms of a mental object or image.

62. rang nyid yin gyis gzhan du ma tshol cig. This line, present in the text of the All-Creating King, is omitted in Longchenpa's citation. It is restored here for the sake of clarity.

63. Longchenpa cites only the first and fourth lines of this stanza. The full stanza (Sūtrālaṃkāra, x, 65) is supplied in the translation for the sake of clarity.

64. Several of Longchenpa's names are worked into the wording of this stanza: tshul khrims blo gros (intelligence of discipline), dri med 'od zer (stainless rays of light), klong chen rab 'byams (all-encompassing expanse).

Texts Cited in *The Chariot*
of *Surpassing Purity*

Abhisamayālaṃkāra: *mNgon rtogs rgyan* (*Ornament of True Realization*). By Maitreya.

Abridged Prajñāpāramitā-sūtra: *Prajñāpāramitāsaṃcayagāthā-sūtra. Phar phyin sdud pa.*

All-Creating King Tantra: *Kun byed rgyal po'i rgyud.*

Arrangement of Samayas: *Dam tshig bkod pa.*

Avataṃsaka-sūtra: *Phal po che.* (*The Ornaments of the Buddha*).

Buddha's Many Deeds Sūtra: *Sangs rgyas mang byed kyi mdo.*

Chariot of Excellence: *Shing rta bzang po*, autocommentary to *Finding Rest in Illusion.* By Longchenpa.

Dawn of Indestructible Light Tantra: *sNang ba rdo rje 'char ba'i rgyud.*

Determination of Valid Knowledge: *Pramāṇaviniścaya. Tshad ma rnam nges.* By Dharmakīrti.

Dohā: *Do ha* (*Songs of Realization*).

Finding Rest in Illusion: *sGyu ma ngal gso.* By Longchenpa.

Garland of the Fortress of Views: *Man ngag lta ba'i rdzong phreng.* Attributed to Padmasambhava.

Glorious Exhaustion of the Four Elements Tantra: *dPal 'byung bzhi zad pa'i rgyud.*

Gradual Path of Secret Mantra: *gSang sngags lam rim.*

Great Chariot: *Shing rta chen po*, autocommentary to *Finding Rest in the Nature of the Mind.* By Longchenpa.

Guhyagarbha Tantra: *gSang ba snying po'i rgyud* (*Secret Essence Tantra*).

Guhyasamāja Tantra: *gSang 'dus* (*Union of Secrets Tantra*).

Hevajra Tantra: *Kye rdo rje'i rgyud.*

Illusory Supreme Bliss Tantra: *sGyu ma bde mchog gi rgyud.*

Kālacakra Root Tantra: *Kālacakramūlatantra. Dus 'khor rtsa rgyud.*

Kālacakra Tantra: *Dus 'khor gyi rgyud* (*Wheel of Time Tantra*).

Lamp for the Path to Enlightenment: *Bodhipathapradīpa. Byang chub lam gyi sgron me.* By Atiśa.

Lotus Crown Tantra: *Pad ma cod pan gyi rgyud.*

Mañjuśrī Tantra: *'Jam dpal gyi rgyud.*

Māyājāla Tantra: *sGyu 'phrul drva ba (Great Net of Illusory Manifestations Tantra).*

Ocean of Primal Wisdom Tantra: *Ye shes rgya mtsho'i rgyud.*

Sūtrālaṃkāra: *mDo sde rgyan (Ornament of Mahāyāna Sūtras).* By Maitreya.

Pledges of the Ḍākinī Tantra: *mKha' 'gro ma'i sdom pa'i rgyud.*

Praise to the Mother: *Yum la bstod pa.*

Prajñāpāramitā in Eight Thousand Lines: *Aṣṭasāhasrikāprajñāpāramitā. brGyad stong pa.*

Prātimokṣa-sūtra: *So sor thar pa'i mdo (Individual Liberation Sūtra).*

Profound Practice of Yoga in the Four Seasons: *Dus bzhi rnal 'byor gyi sgrub pa zab mo.* By Garab Dorje.

Questions of Bhadra the Magician Sūtra: *sGyu ma mkhan bzang pos zhus pa'i mdo.*

Ratnakūṭa-sūtra: *dKon mchog brtsegs pa (Heap of Jewels Sūtra).*

Ratnāvalī: *Rin chen 'phreng ba (Garland of Gems).* By Nāgārjuna.

Sacred Primordial Buddha Tantra: *Dam pa dang po'i rgyud.*

Saṃpuṭa Tantra: *Yang dag par sbyor ba'i rgyud (Perfect Union;* explanatory tantra of Hevajra).

Saṃvarodaya: *sDom 'byung (Tantra of the Emergence of Cakrasamvara).*

Secret Crown Tantra: *gSang ba cod pan gyi rgyud.*

Secret Sphere Tantra: *Thig le gsang ba'i rgyud.*

Sublime Primal Wisdom Tantra: *Ye shes dam pa'i rgyud.*

Supreme Secret Tantra: *gSang ba mchog gi rgyud.*

The Way of the Bodhisattva: *Bodhicaryāvatāra. sPyod 'jug.* By Śāntideva.

The Full Arising of Primal Wisdom Tantra: *Ye shes mngon 'byung gi rgyud.*

Twenty Stanzas on the Bodhichitta Vow: *Samvaravimsaha. sDom pa nyi shu pa.* By Candragomin.

Two-Part Hevajra Tantra: *brTag gnyis* (condensed version of Hevajra Tantra).

Udānavarga: *Ched du brjod pa'i tshoms (Collection of Deliberate Sayings).*

Uttaratantra: *rGyud bla ma (The Sublime Continuum).* By Maitreya.

Vajra Peak Tantra: *Vajraśekhara Tantra, rDo rje rtse mo'i rgyud.*

Vajra Tent Tantra: *Vajrapañjarā Tantra, rDo rje gur gyi rgyud.*

Vast Display Sūtra: *Lalitavistara-sūtra, rGya cher rol pa.*

Victorious Nonduality Tantra: *gNyis med rnam rgyal gyi rgyud.*

INDEX